MARILYN HICKEY MINISTRIES PR

BOOK OF DANIEL

MARILYN HICKEY

Printed in the United States of America
Copyright © 1988, 2013 by Marilyn Hickey
All Rights Reserved

ISBN# 978-1-938696-95-4

CONTENTS

Introduction

This book is the key to future events. The book of Daniel has rightly been called the "Apocalypse of the Old Testament." In the darkest time of Israel's history, Daniel shines as God's prophet to both the gentiles and the Jews. As we shall see, Daniel was given astounding glimpses into the near and distant future—his and ours! One cannot properly understand the New Testament book of Revelation without acquiring knowledge of Daniel's visions and dreams.

Ezekiel and Daniel were contemporaries, and it is obvious that Ezekiel knew about Daniel's godly character:

> *Though these three men, Noah, Daniel, and Job, were in it, they should deliver but their own souls by their righteousness, saith the Lord GOD. Though Noah, Daniel, and Job, were in it, as I live, saith the Lord GOD, they shall deliver neither son nor daughter; they shall but deliver their own souls by their righteousness* (Ezekiel 14:14,20).

Daniel prophesied to the leadership of Babylon while Ezekiel prophesied to the captives held in the 70-year captivity. Daniel and his friends would influence the history of Judah as well as the history of the world.

TEN LESSONS

There are ten outstanding lessons to be learned from Daniel's life and from his book:

1. God disciplines individuals and nations:

NOTES

NOTES

My people are destroyed for lack of knowledge: because thou hast rejected knowledge, I will also reject thee, that thou shalt be no priest to me: seeing thou hast forgotten the law of thy God, I will also forget thy children (Hosea 4:6).

In the third year of the reign of Jehoiakim king of Judah came Nebuchadnezzar king of Babylon unto Jerusalem, and besieged it. And the Lord gave Jehoiakim king of Judah into his hand, with part of the vessels of the house of God: which he carried into the land of Shinar to the house of his god; and he brought the vessels into the treasure house of his god (Daniel 1:1,2).

2. Religion seeks to obscure truth:

Unto whom the prince of the eunuchs gave names: for he gave unto Daniel the name of Belteshazzar; and to Hananiah, of Shadrach; and to Mishael, of Meshach; and to Azariah, of Abednego (Daniel 1:7).

3. Divine viewpoint brings good results:

But Daniel purposed in his heart that he would not defile himself with the portion of the king's meat, nor with the wine which he drank: therefore he requested of the prince of the eunuchs that he might not defile himself (Daniel 1:8).

4. People in high positions tend to be insecure:

And the prince of the eunuchs said unto Daniel, I fear my lord the king, who hath appointed your meat and your drink: for why should he see your faces worse liking than the children which are of your sort? then shall ye make me endanger my head to the king (Daniel 1:10).

5. Perception of doctrine makes academic perception easier:

As for these four children, God gave them knowledge and skill in all learning and wisdom: and Daniel had understanding in all visions and dreams. And the king communed with them; and among them all was found none like Daniel, Hananiah, Mishael, and Azariah: therefore stood they before the king (Daniel 1:17,19).

6. God honors those who put His Word first:

As for these four children, God gave them knowledge and skill in all learning and wisdom: and Daniel had understanding in all visions and dreams. And the king communed with them; and among them all was found none like Daniel, Hananiah, Mishael, and Azariah: therefore stood they before the king (Daniel 1:17,19).

7. God uses prepared people:

And in all matters of wisdom and understanding, that the king enquired of them, he found them ten times better than all the magicians and astrologers that were in all his realm (Daniel 1:20).

8. God honors faithfulness:

And Daniel continued even unto the first year of king Cyrus (Daniel 1:21).

NOTES

3

9. God never leaves Himself without a witness:

And in all matters of wisdom and understanding, that the king enquired of them, he found them ten times better than all the magicians and astrologers that were in all his realm. And Daniel continued even unto the first year of king Cyrus (Daniel 1:20,21).

10. Premium is placed on character:

Then this Daniel was preferred above the presidents and princes, because an excellent spirit was in him; and the king thought to set him over the whole realm (Daniel 6:3).

FIVE EMPIRES

There are five empires that we should keep in mind as we study the book of Daniel:

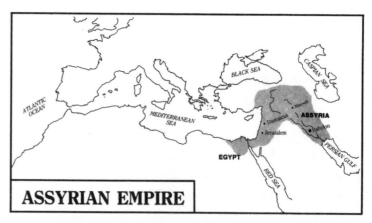

ASSYRIAN EMPIRE

1. **ASSYRIA**—They led the northern ten tribes captive after attacking Samaria around 722 B.C. Nineveh, the eventual capital of Assyria, was founded by Asshur, a son of Shem:

Out of that land went forth Asshur, and builded Nineveh, and the city Rehoboth, and Calah (Genesis 10:11).

*The children of Shem; Elam, and
Asshur, and Arphaxad, and Lud, and
Aram* (Genesis 10:22).

Nineveh became the capital of Assyria in 1270 B.C.
The Assyrian kings also became the masters of Chaldea
or Babylon.

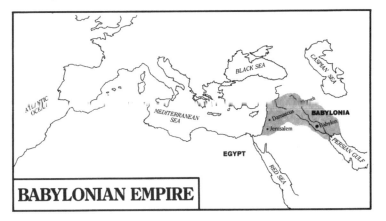

BABYLONIAN EMPIRE

2. **BABYLON**—The father of Babylon was Nimrod, a
   Hamite and the great-grandson of Noah. Babylon
   was founded over 2,000 years before Christ:

   *And Cush begat Nimrod: he began to be
   a mighty one in the earth. He was a
   mighty hunter before the LORD:
   wherefore it is said, Even as Nimrod the
   mighty hunter before the LORD. And the
   beginning of his kingdom was Babel,
   and Erech, and Accad, and Calneh, in
   the land of Shinar* (Genesis 10:8-10).

In 720 B.C. Berodach-Baladan (also spelled Merodach-
Baladan) became king of Babylon and sent ambassadors
to Hezekiah (see II Kings 20:12-18, Isaiah 39:1-7). In 625
B.C., Berodach-Baladan's son, Nabopolassar (the father
of Nebuchadnezzar) overthrew the Assyrians and brought
Babylon to greatness. Nebuchadnezzar, in turn, made
Babylon famous by building the "hanging gardens" for
his homesick wife and by erecting the tower of Bel. The
prophet Isaiah spoke of Babylon's prominence and its
eventual ruin:

NOTES

5

And Babylon, the glory of kingdoms, the beauty of the Chaldees' excellency, shall be as when God overthrew Sodom and Gomorrah (Isaiah 13:19).

Babylon is mentioned in twelve other books of the Old Testament (II Kings; I & II Chronicles, Ezra, Nehemiah, Esther, Psalms, Isaiah, Jeremiah, Ezekiel, Micah, and Zechariah) and four books of the New Testament (Matthew, Acts, I Peter, and Revelation).

There were three invasions of Judah by the Babylonians:

a. After a stunning defeat of Egypt, Babylon invaded Jerusalem, and Daniel was taken into captivity along with his three friends. In this captivity Jehoia**chin** (Jehoia**kim**'s son) was left on the throne in Jerusalem.

b. In 598 B.C. the second invasion occurred. Ezekiel and Jehoiachin were numbered among the captives.

c. During the third invasion Nebuchadnezzar besieged Jerusalem for 18 months; it finally fell in 586 B.C., ending in the third deportation. The people of Judah had entered into the 5th cycle of discipline (Leviticus 26:33) which lasted for 70 years.

PERSIAN EMPIRE

3. **MEDO-PERSIA**—Around 539 B.C. Cyrus the Persian, after conquering the Medes, defeated the Babylonians and allowed the Jews to return to their homeland. Daniel was still active in Babylon through the time of Cyrus:

And Daniel continued even unto the first year of king Cyrus (Daniel 1:21).

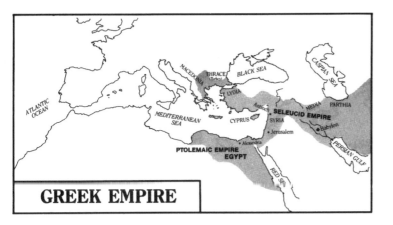

GREEK EMPIRE

4. **GREECE**—Alexander the Great defeated the Persian Empire around 331 B.C. Greek culture and ideas were still present during the time of Christ and the apostles. After the day of Pentecost, a conflict occurred between Greek and Hebrew Christians:

And in those days, when the number of the disciples was multiplied, there arose a murmuring of the Grecians against the Hebrews, because their widows were neglected in the daily ministration (Acts 6:1).

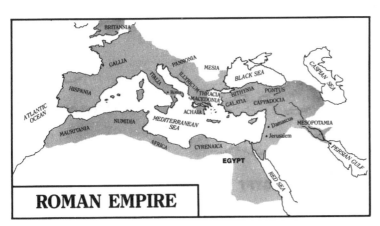

ROMAN EMPIRE

5. **ROME**—The Roman Empire was founded in 753 B.C. and spread its domain over most of the known world by the time of Christ.

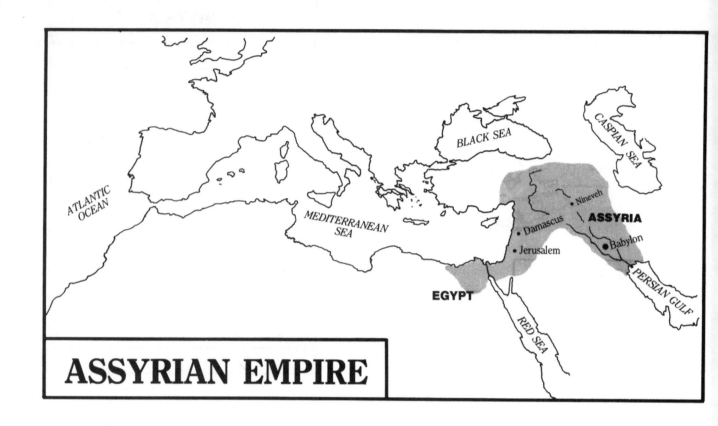

ASSYRIAN EMPIRE

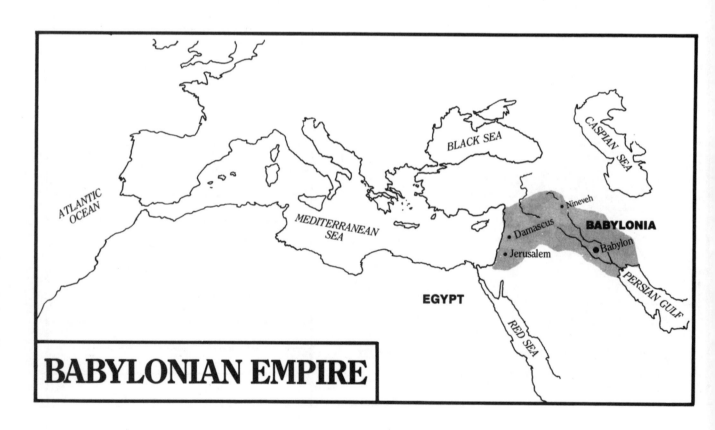

BABYLONIAN EMPIRE

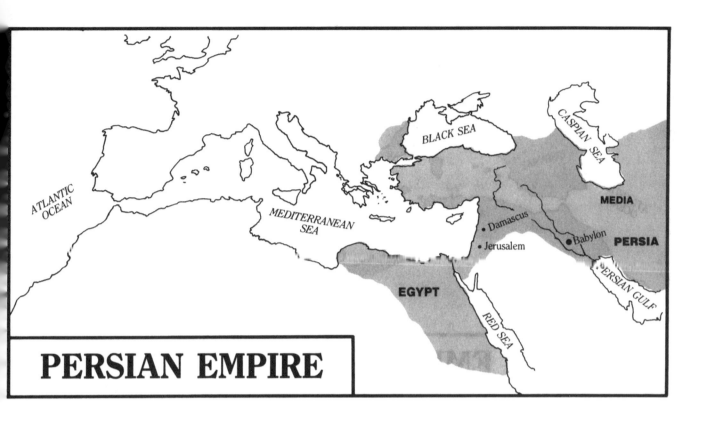

PERSIAN EMPIRE

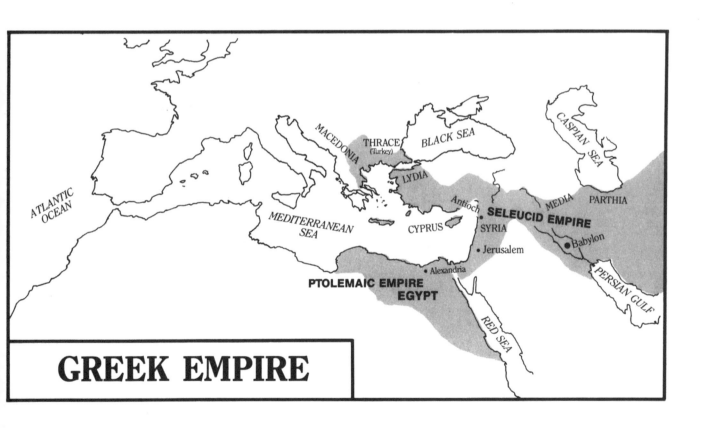

GREEK EMPIRE

9

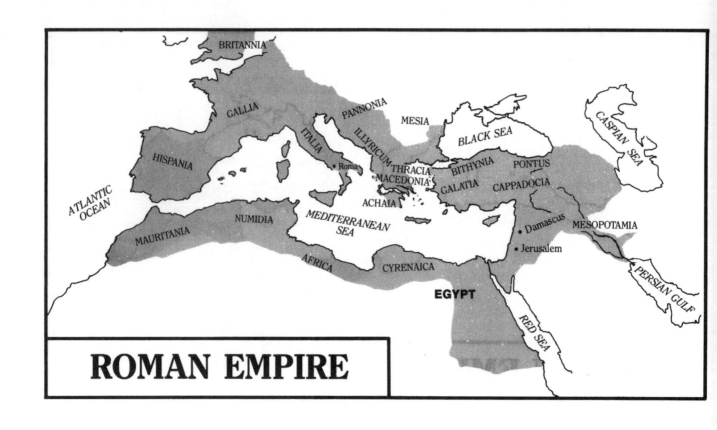

ROMAN EMPIRE

CHAPTER ONE

Daniel's First Adventures in Babylon

Daniel is given some excellent titles by the Lord. He is called a man greatly beloved (Daniel 9:23), and he is also called a man of excellent spirit (Daniel 6:3). If we were describing Daniel, we would probably say he was Spirit-dominated. He excelled in being Spirit-dominated. He was fair and strong and physical. But what dominated his being was the Spirit of God. He was a man who lived life in the Spirit and from that center governed the material realm.

In chapter one we see brainwashing—Chaldean style. They changed the names of Daniel and his three friends, thinking that would change their character:

Azariah, which means "Jehovah aids," had his name changed to *Abednego*, meaning "servant of Nebo," a Chaldean god.

Hananiah means "Jehovah is gracious." His name was changed to *Shadrach*, which was one of the names of the Chaldean idols.

Mishael means "who is like God." His name was changed to *Meshach*, which was another name of a Chaldean idol.

Daniel means "God is judge," but his name was changed to *Belteshazzar*, meaning "Bel protects his life."

There are four basic things that you will see in Daniel's life:
1. He was a man of PURPOSE.
2. He was a man of PRAYER.
3. He was a man of PERCEPTION.
4. He was a man of POWER.

PURPOSE

Immediately in chapter one we see that Daniel PURPOSED in his heart that he wouldn't defile himself with the king's meat. Purpose is wonderful—it anchors you in time of temptation and is a stronghold in battle. Find God's purpose and everything else will fall in place. Daniel found it, named it his own, announced it to others, and stood by it in adversity.

We need to find our purpose. What was Daniel's purpose? His purpose was not to defile himself. He made that known at the beginning, and that purpose influenced all his actions.

Daniel and his friends, along with the others in the king's court, were evidently required to eat meat offered to idols. Daniel purposed in his heart not to defile himself by eating such food. He asked the head of the eunuchs if he and his friends could eat a diet that was fitting for them for ten days. If, at the end of the ten days, they didn't look better than those on the king's diet, Daniel and his friends would go back to the diet of King Nebuchadnezzar.

When we purpose in our hearts, God begins to put the pieces of our lives together. God gave Daniel favor with the prince of the eunuchs and honored Daniel's determination to keep himself undefiled:

> *And at the end of ten days their countenances appeared fairer and fatter in flesh than all the children which did eat the portion of the king's meat* (Daniel 1:15).

These four young men had knowledge and skill in all learning and wisdom. Daniel had understanding in visions. Purposing in your heart pays rich rewards!

Daniel was not the only one to receive his training in a palace—so had Joseph and Moses.

Daniel and his friends could have had a feast or they could have had their faith—they chose faith over feast. Daniel was a man who had purposed and prepared his heart. God honors not only faith—He honors faithfulness. Daniel received a place of high honor and became a favorite and a leader in the Medo-Persian empire which took over Babylon. Please note the premium which was placed on Daniel's character.

PRAYER

Because Daniel purposed in his heart to serve God, he was a person of PRAYER. Later in this book we see that Daniel prayed three times each day:

> *Now when Daniel knew that the writing was signed, he went into his house; and his windows being open in his chamber toward Jerusalem, he kneeled upon his*

13

NOTES

*knees three times a day, and prayed, and
gave thanks before his God, as he did
aforetime* (Daniel 6:10).

When Daniel was persecuted for his commitment to
prayer, he still didn't give it up even though it meant his
life was on the line:

*All the presidents of the kingdom, the
governors, and the princes, the
counsellors, and captains, have consulted
together to establish a royal statute, and to
make a firm decree, that whosoever shall
ask a petition of any God or man for
thirty days, save of thee, O king, he
shall be cast into the den of lions* (Daniel 6:7).

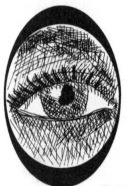

PERCEPTION

Out of his prayer Daniel began to get spiritual PERCEPTION.
When King Nebuchadnezzar threatened to kill all the wise
men in the land because none could tell him his dream or
its meaning, Daniel requested time to pray and seek the
answer from God:

*Then Daniel went to his house, and made
the thing known to Hananiah, Mishael,
and Azariah, his companions: That they
would desire mercies of the God of
heaven concerning this secret; that Daniel
and his fellows should not perish with
the rest of the wise men of Babylon*
(Daniel 2:17,18).

POWER

This was just the first of many visions and their interpretations that were given to Daniel. Out of his great spiritual perception came POWER with the rulers of Babylon:

The king answered unto Daniel, and said, Of a truth it is, that your God is a God of gods, and a Lord of kings, and a revealer of secrets, seeing thou couldest reveal this secret. Then the king made Daniel a great man, and gave him many great gifts, and made him ruler over the whole province of Babylon, and chief of the governors over all the wise men of Babylon (Daniel 2:47,48).

NOTES

CHAPTER TWO
A Troubled King

We know that Nebuchadnezzar had been chosen for his kingship:

> *. . . Thus saith the LORD of hosts, the God of Israel; Thus shall ye say unto your masters; I have made the earth, the man and the beast that are upon the ground, by my great power and by my outstretched arm, and have given it unto whom it seemed meet unto me. And now have I given all these lands into the hand of Nebuchadnezzar the king of Babylon, my servant; and the beasts of the field have I given him also to serve him.*

> *And all nations shall serve him, and his son, and his son's son, until the very time of his land come: and then many nations and great kings shall serve themselves of him. And it shall come to pass, that the nation and kingdom which will not serve the same Nebuchadnezzar the king of Babylon, and that will not put their neck under the yoke of the king of Babylon, that nation will I punish, saith the LORD, with the sword, and with the famine, and with the pestilence, until I have consumed them by his hand* (Jeremiah 27:4-8).

Religion always seeks to obscure truth, but God has a way of getting through to men. Nebuchadnezzar had a dream that bothered him; he could not shake the dream, yet he did not remember the details of the dream.

NOTES

17

Nebuchadnezzar went to his "wise men"—at least they were wise enough to know that unless they had a spiritual revelation, they could not know the king's dream:

The Chaldeans answered before the king, and said, There is not a man upon the earth that can shew the king's matter: therefore there is no king, lord, nor ruler, that asked such things at any magician, or astrologer, or Chaldean. And it is a rare thing the king requireth, and there is none other that can shew it before the king, except the gods, whose dwelling is not with flesh (Daniel 2:10,11).

The king had been footing the bill for all the magicians and "wise men" in his court, so you can imagine his anger when they couldn't tell him what he had dreamed or its meaning. He ordered all the wise men in Babylon to be killed, which included Daniel and his three friends:

For this cause the king was angry and very furious, and commanded to destroy all the wise men of Babylon (Daniel 2:12).

Fortunately for Daniel, he was not only a man of purpose, but he was also a man of prayer. He called his friends together for an all-night prayer meeting:

Then Daniel went to his house, and made the thing known to Hananiah, Mishael, and Azariah, his companions: That they

18

*would desire mercies of the God of heaven
concerning this secret; that Daniel and
his fellows should not perish with the rest
of the wise men of Babylon* (Daniel 2:17,18).

Daniel already had a regular habit of prayer; later we
see that he prayed three times a day (Daniel 6:10). Strong
purposes cannot stand without prayer.

What is prayer? Basically it is our time of weakness but
God's time of power. It shows our limitation but God's
sufficiency. God and Daniel were stronger than all of the
Chaldean corruption, all of the Babylonian corruption, and
all of the corruption of the Medes and the Persians. Daniel
was *in* the world but not *of* the world.

God's wisdom prevails over idolatrous evil. When you
link up with God, the two of you are invincible against all
of the forces that come against you. When Daniel heard
the news that all the wise men were to be killed because
they could not reveal the dream or its interpretation, he
had an all-night prayer meeting that would make history.
The way to make good history is to have all-night prayer
meetings!

After Daniel received a revelation of Nebuchadnezzar's
dream, he blessed the Lord and gave Him all the credit
and all the glory:

> *Then was the secret revealed unto Daniel
> in a night vision. Then Daniel blessed the
> God of heaven. Daniel answered and
> said, Blessed be the name of God for
> ever and ever: for wisdom and might are
> his: And he changeth the times and the
> seasons: he removeth kings, and setteth
> up kings: he giveth wisdom unto the wise,
> and knowledge to them that know under-
> standing: He revealeth the deep and
> secret things: he knoweth what is in the
> darkness, and the light dwelleth with him.
> I thank thee, and praise thee, O thou
> God of my fathers, who hast given me
> wisdom and might, and hast made known*

NOTES

unto me now what we desired of thee: for thou hast now made known unto us the king's matter (Daniel 2:19-23).

The king's vision was for a "latter day":

But there is a God in heaven that revealeth secrets, and maketh known to the king Nebuchadnezzar what shall be in the latter days. Thy dream, and visions of thy head upon thy bed, are these (Daniel 2:28).

Verse 28 is a real key to what follows; the vision has to do with secrets of the "latter days." We are living in those latter days!

Nebuchadnezzar's dream concerns itself with the time of the gentiles. The time of the gentiles began at the time when Daniel was taken into captivity.

Let's look at Nebuchadnezzar's image and Daniel's interpretation:

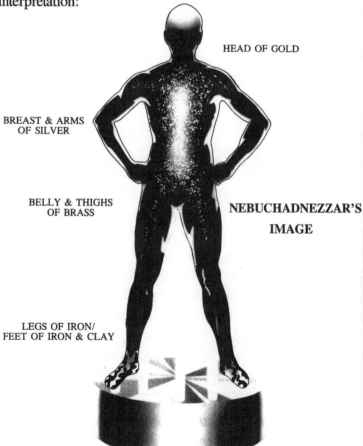

HEAD OF GOLD

BREAST & ARMS OF SILVER

BELLY & THIGHS OF BRASS

LEGS OF IRON/ FEET OF IRON & CLAY

NEBUCHADNEZZAR'S IMAGE

Thou, O king, sawest, and behold a great image. This great image, whose brightness was excellent, stood before thee; and the form thereof was terrible. This image's head was of fine gold, his breast and his arms of silver, his belly and his thighs of brass, His legs of iron, his feet part of iron and part of clay (Daniel 2:31-33).

THE HEAD OF GOLD
Babylonian

We do not need to guess about the meaning of this image; Daniel was also given the interpretation of the vision:

Thou, O king, art a king of kings: for the God of heaven hath given thee a kingdom, power and strength, and glory. And wheresoever the children of men dwell, the beasts of the field and the fowls of the heaven hath he given into thine hand, and hath made thee ruler over them all. Thou art this head of gold (Daniel 2:37,38).

Notice that each one of the elements composing the image is inferior to the one preceding it. Gold is followed by silver, the silver is followed by brass, the brass is followed by iron, and the iron is followed by clay. The head of gold represents the Babylonian empire—superior to all those empires that followed it:

And Babylon, the glory of kingdoms, the beauty of the Chaldees' excellency, shall be as when God overthrew Sodom and Gomorrah (Isaiah 13:19).

NOTES

NOTES

THE BREAST AND ARMS OF SILVER
Medo-Persian

And after thee shall arise another kingdom inferior to thee, . . . (Daniel 2:39).

It was prophesied that the Medes and the Persians would take over the Babylonian Empire:

That saith of Cyrus, He is my shepherd, and shall perform all my pleasure: even saying to Jerusalem, Thou shalt be built; and to the temple, Thy foundation shall be laid. Thus saith the LORD to his anointed, to Cyrus, whose right hand I have holden, to subdue nations before him; and I will loose the loins of kings, to open before him the two leaved gates; and the gates shall not be shut;

I will go before thee, and make the crooked places straight: I will break in pieces the gates of brass, and cut in sunder the bars of iron: And I will give thee the treasures of darkness, and hidden riches of secret places, that thou mayest know that I, the LORD, which call thee by thy name, am the God of Israel. For Jacob my servant's sake, and Israel mine elect, I have even called thee by thy name: I have surnamed thee, though thou hast not known me
(Isaiah 44:28-45:4).

How interesting that Cyrus was prenamed over 100 years before his birth, and a description of portions of Babylon was given before it was even built!

This second world empire had two parts, as indicated by the two arms of silver. Two nations united to conquer Babylon: the Persians and the Medes. Today these empires would comprise the area around Iran and Iraq.

THE BELLY AND THIGHS OF BRASS
Grecian

. . . and another third kingdom of brass, which shall bear rule over all the earth (Daniel 2:39).

The third empire (of which we will see more in Daniel 8) was brass, which is inferior to silver. The Greek Empire would overcome the Medes and the Persians and later would be divided among four generals after the death of Alexander the Great. The modern-day division of the Greek Empire would be Greece, Turkey, Syria, and part of Africa.

THE LEGS OF IRON WITH FEET OF IRON AND CLAY
Roman

23

NOTES

And the fourth kingdom shall be strong as iron: forasmuch as iron breaketh in pieces and subdueth all things: and as iron that breaketh all these, shall it break in pieces and bruise. And whereas thou sawest the feet and toes, part of potters' clay, and part of iron, the kingdom shall be divided; but there shall be in it of the strength of the iron, forasmuch as thou sawest the iron mixed with miry clay (Daniel 2:40,41).

The fourth empire, the Roman, is not named as such in the book of Daniel—but undoubtedly this is what it is. Rome would govern with an *iron* rule. It would be an empire that would take up a great deal of the image, at least half of it, because of its long legs. We see two legs, and we know that the Roman Empire was divided into the Eastern and Western empires. We know also that the ten toes represent ten kingdoms. Some would be dominated by dictatorship and some by a more democratic type of government.

In the end-time the Antichrist will rise again from the area of the old Roman Empire. Undoubtedly he will have ten nations who give honor unto him, but in the vision a stone crushes the image:

Thou sawest till that a stone was cut out without hands, which smote the image upon his feet that were of iron and clay, and brake them to pieces. Then was the iron, the clay, the brass, the silver, and the gold, broken to pieces together, and became like the chaff of the summer threshingfloors; and the wind carried them away, that no place was found for them: and the stone that smote the image became a great mountain, and filled the whole earth (Daniel 2:34,35).

We know Who that Rock is—that is the Lord Jesus Christ:

Wherefore also it is contained in scripture,

24

Behold, I lay in Sion a chief corner
stone, elect, precious: and he that
believeth on him shall not be confounded.
Unto you therefore which believe he is
precious: but unto them which be disobedient,
the stone which the builders disallowed,
the same is made the head of the corner,
And a stone of stumbling, and a rock of
offence, at the word, being disobedient:
whereunto also they were appointed
(I Peter 2:6-8).

When King Nebuchadnezzar heard from Daniel the
dream and its interpretation, he responded with insight that
reveals the Trinity:

The king answered unto Daniel, and said,
Of a truth it is, that your God is a God
of gods, and a Lord of kings, and a
revealer of secrets, seeing thou couldest
reveal this secret (Daniel 2:47).

Truly our heavenly Father is the God of gods, our Jesus
is the Lord of kings, and the wonderful Holy Spirit is the
revealer of secrets.

Daniel, the man of purpose, was also a man of prayer.
Then he became a man of perception. We always want
spiritual perception, but until we have purpose and prayer,
we do not receive the perception. Daniel's reward was
tremendous:

Then the king made Daniel a great man,
and gave him many great gifts, and made
him ruler over the whole province of
Babylon, and chief of the governors over
all the wise men of Babylon. Then Daniel
requested of the king, and he set Shadrach,
Meshach, and Abednego, over the affairs
of the province of Babylon: but Daniel sat
in the gate of the king (Daniel 2:48,49).

NOTES

NOTES

Now Daniel had become a man of power. Power can never come except out of prayer—then it gives glory to God and not to man.

CHAPTER THREE
A Miraculous Deliverance

Many years separate the events of chapter two and chapter three. Nebuchadnezzar returned to Jerusalem to put down further rebellion and burned the city, destroying the Temple. Apparently this victory lulled him into thinking that the Jewish God was not all-powerful after all.

Nebuchadnezzar hadn't, however, forgotten his dream of the great image with its head of gold representing himself. His empire had grown over the years, and Nebuchadnezzar fell into the old carnal, humanistic, secular plan to unite the empire through one religion. The Roman Empire tried to use the same tactic; it was OK to worship and serve any idol or god you chose, but one day each year you had to offer a pinch of incense to Caesar. That was their way of saying that Caesar was divine, and if they could get the people thinking that Caesar was divine, obedience would follow. The Caesar's word would then be the Word of God.

But no human being is ever God speaking unless he is speaking the Word of God. Man is not God, but man has the ability to speak God's Word.

Nebuchadnezzar sought to unify his empire by making a huge image:

> *Nebuchadnezzar the king made an image of gold, whose height was threescore cubits, and the breadth thereof six cubits: he set it up in the plain of Dura, in the province of Babylon* (Daniel 3:1).

NOTES

<table>
<tr><th colspan="2" style="text-align:center">NOTES</th></tr>
<tr><td></td></tr>
<tr><td></td></tr>
<tr><td></td></tr>
<tr><td></td></tr>
<tr><td></td></tr>
<tr><td></td></tr>
<tr><td></td></tr>
<tr><td></td></tr>
<tr><td></td></tr>
<tr><td></td></tr>
<tr><td></td></tr>
<tr><td></td></tr>
<tr><td></td></tr>
<tr><td></td></tr>
<tr><td></td></tr>
<tr><td></td></tr>
<tr><td></td></tr>
<tr><td></td></tr>
<tr><td></td></tr>
<tr><td></td></tr>
<tr><td></td></tr>
<tr><td></td></tr>
<tr><td></td></tr>
<tr><td></td></tr>
<tr><td></td></tr>
</table>

This image was 60 cubits high (about 90 feet) and 6 cubits wide (about 9 feet). It is more than coincidence that this image involves the number six. Six is the number of man, and 666 is the number of the Satanic trinity mentioned in Revelation:

> *Here is wisdom. Let him that hath understanding count the number of the beast: for it is the number of a man; and his number is Six hundred threescore and six* (Revelation 13:18).

There is no doubt that the three Hebrew children knew of God's promise to them penned many years earlier by the prophet Isaiah:

> *When thou passest through the waters, I will be with thee; and through the rivers, they shall not overflow thee: when thou*

walkest through the fire, thou shalt not be burned; neither shall the flame kindle upon thee (Isaiah 43:2).

Because of their faith, Shadrach, Meshach, and Abednego are found in the New Testament hall of fame of faith:

Who through faith . . . Quenched the violence of fire, . . . (Hebrews 11:33,34).

How did they do it? Through faith! What is the word they stood on? Isaiah 43:2.

Nebuchadnezzar set up his image in the plain of Dura. What was he doing? He was making himself God. All the leaders of his vast empire were invited to the dedication of this idolatrous image and ordered to bow to the image, which really meant acknowledging that Nebuchadnezzar was supreme:

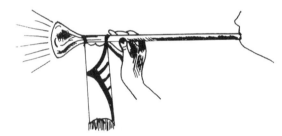

Then an herald cried aloud, To you it is commanded, O people, nations, and languages, That at what time ye hear the sound of the cornet, flute, harp, sackbut, psaltery, dulcimer, and all kinds of musick, ye fall down and worship the golden image that Nebuchadnezzar the king hath set up (Daniel 3:4,5).

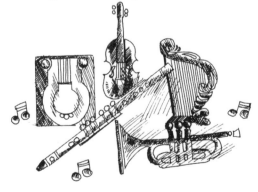

NOTES

NOTES

I don't know where Daniel was at this time, but I have a feeling that he was out of town on business for the king. We know that he wouldn't have bowed to the image, because he had already purposed in his heart not to defile himself.

King Nebuchadnezzar must have had a feeling that there were some within his empire who would see through what he was doing and refuse to acknowledge him as deity. He had already thought of one way to exert a little pressure on his subjects to worship his image:

> *And whoso falleth not down and worshippeth shall the same hour be cast into the midst of a burning fiery furnace* (Daniel 3:6).

But the Hebrew children said, "We can't bow down to idols. We can't do that. We don't believe Nebuchadnezzar is God. We believe there is one God." The law of the Hebrews forbade them to worship an idol:

> *Thou shalt not make unto thee any graven image, or any likeness of any thing that is in heaven above, or that is in the earth beneath, or that is in the water under the earth: Thou shalt not bow down thyself to them, nor serve them: for I the LORD thy God am a jealous God, visiting the iniquity of the fathers upon the children unto the third and fourth generation of them that hate me; And shewing mercy unto thousands of them that love me, and keep my commandments* (Exodus 20:4-6).

When it was told to Nebuchadnezzar that the three Jews had refused to bow to the golden image, you can imagine how embarrassed that made Nebuchadnezzar in front of all his officials, rulers, and counselors! He ordered that Shadrach, Meshach, and Abed-nego be brought before him:

> *Then Nebuchadnezzar in his rage and fury commanded to bring Shadrach, Meshach, and Abed-nego. Then they brought these men before the king* (Daniel 3:13).

30

The king was at least willing to give them one more chance to change their minds and worship the image. If they refused again, Nebuchadnezzar promised to have them thrown into the fiery furnace *within the hour!*

I love what the three Hebrews said to the king:

> *If it be so, our God whom we serve is able to deliver us from the burning fiery furnace, and he will deliver us out of thine hand, O king. But if not, be it known unto thee, O king, that we will not serve thy gods, nor worship the golden image which thou hast set up* (Daniel 3:17,18).

Now that's PURE PURPOSE. We put too many "ifs" on God: "*If* You save my husband, then I'll really serve You," "*If* You get me out of this trouble, then I'll give my life to You." That's manipulation! Drop it, and say, "God, I'm Yours, PERIOD!"

These three young men knew the promise of God in Isaiah 43:2. They had faith that God would deliver them. "But," they said, "*if* for any reason God doesn't deliver us, we still won't worship your image!" THERE IS NO WAY YOU CAN LOSE WITH THAT KIND OF FAITH:

> *Though he slay me, yet will I trust in him:* . . . (Job 13:15).

That kind of "fanaticism" infuriates the world. Unbelievers can't comprehend that kind of commitment. Look at the reaction of the king to such mountain-moving faith:

> *Then was Nebuchadnezzar full of fury, and the form of his visage was changed against Shadrach, Meshach, and Abednego: therefore he spake, and commanded that they should heat the furnace one seven times more than it was wont to be heated* (Daniel 3:19).

NOTES

Fury always leads to folly. If Nebuchadnezzar had wanted to increase the punishment for the three Hebrews, he should have *lowered* the fire rather than *increase* its intensity. The king's anger only succeeded in killing the men who threw the three Jews into the fire:

> *Therefore because the king's commandment was urgent, and the furnace exceeding hot, the flame of the fire slew those men that took up Shadrach, Meshach, and Abed-nego* (Daniel 3:22).

Most likely the "furnace" was a large hole in the ground. Normally criminals were stripped before being executed, but in Nebuchadnezzar's rage he had the men *". . . bound in their coats, their hosen, and their hats, and their other garments, . . ."* before throwing them into the fire (Daniel 3:21). The king's senselessness, however, only worked to the greater glory of God!

Nebuchadnezzar had the best seat available to see his vengeful punishment carried out upon the three young men. Instead of ending their lives, however, the fire freed the Israelites from their bonds and gave them an experience with the Lord that they would never forget:

> *Then Nebuchadnezzar the king was astonied, and rose up in haste, and spake, and said unto his counsellors, Did not we cast three men bound into the midst of the fire? They answered and said unto the king, True, O king. He answered and said, Lo, I see four men loose, walking*

in the midst of the fire, and they have no
hurt; and the form of the fourth is like
the Son of God (Daniel 3:24,25).

Who was the fourth person? It was Jesus! It was
Jehovah-Shammah— "the Lord is there," because He never
left! God is with you, even when you face death:

Yea, though I walk through the valley of
the shadow of death, I will fear no evil:
for thou art with me; thy rod and thy
staff they comfort me (Psalms 23:4).

Notice that Shadrach, Meshach, and Abed-nego weren't
in any hurry to come out of the fire—Nebuchadnezzar had
to call them out. *This* time they obeyed:

Then Nebuchadnezzar came near to the
mouth of the burning fiery furnace, and
spake, and said, Shadrach, Meshach, and
Abed-nego, ye servants of the most high
God, come forth, and come hither. Then
Shadrach, Meshach, and Abed-nego, came
forth of the midst of the fire (Daniel 3:26).

Nothing demonstrates the total and complete salvation of
our God more than the condition of these three men after
they emerged from the flames and ashes of the fiery pit:

And the princes, governors, and captains,
and the king's counsellors, being gathered
together, saw these men, upon whose
bodies the fire had no power, nor was an
hair of their head singed, neither were
their coats changed, nor the smell of fire
had passed on them (Daniel 3:27).

Hallelujah! They came out without so much as the *smell*
of fire on them! This astounding display of the true God's
power to save and deliver softened the proud and hardened
heart of the king:

Then Nebuchadnezzar spake, and said,
blessed be the God of Shadrach,

33

NOTES

NOTES

Meshach, and Abed-nego, who hath sent his angel, and delivered his servants that trusted in him and have changed the king's word, and yielded their bodies, that they might not serve nor worship any god, except their own God.

Therefore I make a decree, That every people, nation, and language, which speak anything amiss against the God of Shadrach, Meshach, and Abed-nego, shall be cut in pieces, and their houses shall be made a dunghill: because there is no other God that can deliver after this sort (Daniel 3:28,29).

At the end of chapter two we saw that Daniel sat in the gate of the king—meaning he had a place of great honor. Now, at the end of chapter three, we see that the faith and purpose of the three Israelites brought them increased power:

Then the king promoted Shadrach, Meshach, and Abed-nego, in the province of Babylon (Daniel 3:30).

Those three men came out better than when they went in. God will exalt you in the middle of your enemies if you commit unreservedly to Him:

Thou preparest a table before me in the presence of mine enemies: thou anointest my head with oil; my cup runneth over (Psalms 23:5).

The anointing and POWER of God are waiting for anyone who will PURPOSE in his heart to serve Him, PRAY without ceasing for God's will to be done, and PERCEIVE in the spirit the answers that follow. Truly their cup ran over—and so can yours!

CHAPTER FOUR
A Converted King

This chapter is the personal conversion testimony of the most powerful man on earth during his time. It is a beautiful story of the first gentile world emperor converted through the prayers of the very slaves he had taken captive many years earlier.

Nebuchadnezzar means "broken ceramic," and we might say that he was a "cracked pot" whom God restored. We will see a man who literally lost his mind and had it restored when he lifted up his eyes to God. When we get to heaven, we will meet and talk with King Nebuchadnezzar!

Daniel 4:1-3 is considered a Babylonian state document. It is a proclamation of King Nebuchadnezzar to the whole world. History records that it was issued in 562 B.C.—the year Nebuchadnezzar recovered from his insanity and just one year before his death:

> *Nebuchadnezzar the king, unto all people, nations, and languages, that dwell in all the earth; Peace be multiplied unto you. I thought it good to shew the signs and wonders that the high God hath wrought toward me. How great are his signs! and how mighty are his wonders! his kingdom is an everlasting kingdom, and his dominion is from generation to generation* (Daniel 4:1-3).

God spoke to Nebuchadnezzar through dreams. God deals with men through their dreams when He cannot get their attention in the daylight hours:

NOTES

NOTES

For God speaketh once, yea twice, yet man perceiveth it not. In a dream, in a vision of the night, when deep sleep falleth upon men, in slumberings upon the bed; Then he openeth the ears of men, and sealeth their instruction, That he may withdraw man from his purpose, and hide pride from man. He keepeth back his soul from the pit, and his life from perishing by the sword (Job 33:14-18).

Nebuchadnezzar's testimony begins with a dream:

I Nebuchadnezzar was at rest in mine house, and flourishing in my palace: I saw a dream which made me afraid, and the thoughts upon my bed and the visions of my head troubled me (Daniel 4:4,5).

The king sought to have his "wise" men interpret the dream, but once again they were helpless to come up with the dream's meaning. At last Daniel came before the king, and Nebuchadnezzar had to acknowledge that the Spirit of God in Daniel could provide the meaning of the dream:

But at the last Daniel came in before me, whose name was Belteshazzar, according to the name of my god, and in whom is the spirit of the holy gods: and before him I told the dream, saying, O Belteshazzar, master of the magicians, because I know that the spirit of the holy gods is in thee, and no secret troubleth thee, tell me the visions of my dream that I have seen, and the interpretation thereof (Daniel 4:8,9).

Let's take a close look at Nebuchadnezzar's vision:

Thus were the visions of mine head in my bed; I saw, and behold a tree in the midst of the earth, and the height thereof was great. The tree grew, and was strong, and the height thereof reached unto

heaven, and the sight thereof to the end
of all the earth: The leaves thereof were
fair, and the fruit thereof much, and in it
was meat for all: the beasts of the field
had shadow under it, and the fowls of the
heaven dwelt in the boughs thereof, and
all flesh was fed of it (Daniel 4:10-12).

Daniel was speechless for an hour after he heard the dream. He didn't want to tell the king the unpleasant interpretation, but Nebuchadnezzar finally prompted him to reveal it:

The tree that thou sawest . . . It is thou,
O king, that art grown and become
strong: for thy greatness is grown, and
reacheth unto heaven, and thy dominion
to the end of the earth (Daniel 4:20,22).

The Bible often uses trees to describe great men:

And Jehoash the king of Israel sent to
Amaziah king of Judah, saying, The thistle
that was in Lebanon sent to the cedar
that was in Lebanon, saying, Give thy
daughter to my son to wife: and there
passed by a wild beast that was in
Lebanon, and trode down the thistle
(II Kings 14:9).

NOTES

Blessed is the man that walketh not in the counsel of the ungodly, . . . he shall be like a tree planted by the rivers of water, that bringeth forth his fruit in his season; his leaf also shall not wither; and whatsoever he doeth shall prosper (Psalms 1:1,3).

But I am like a green olive tree in the house of God: I trust in the mercy of God for ever and ever (Psalms 52:8).

The righteous shall flourish like the palm tree: he shall grow like a cedar in Lebanon (Psalms 92:12).

Behold, the Assyrian was a cedar in Lebanon with fair branches, and with a shadowing shroud, and of an high stature; and his top was among the thick boughs. Therefore his height was exalted above all the trees of the field, and his boughs were multiplied, and his branches became long because of the multitude of waters, when he shot forth (Ezekiel 31:3,5).

Following his vision of the tree, Nebuchadnezzar saw an angel descend and issue a decree concerning the tree:

He cried aloud, and said thus, Hew down the tree, and cut off his branches, shake off his leaves, and scatter his fruit: let the beasts get away from under it, and the fowls from his branches: Nevertheless leave the stump of his roots in the earth, even with a band of iron and brass, in the tender grass of the field; and let it be wet with the dew of heaven, and let his portion be with the beasts in the grass of the earth: Let his heart be changed from man's, and let a beast's heart be given unto him; and let seven times pass over him (Daniel 4:14-16).

The tree was to be cut down and bound with iron and brass, perhaps symbolic of the judgment of madness that would bind Nebuchadnezzar. We see later that it was pride that brought Nebuchadnezzar low:

> *The king spake, and said, Is not this great Babylon, that I have built for the house of the kingdom by the might of my power, and for the honour of my majesty? While the word was in the king's mouth, there fell a voice from heaven, saying, O king Nebuchadnezzar, to thee it is spoken; The kingdom is departed from thee* (Daniel 4:30,31).

Leadership can sometimes get into a very high pride level. Pharaoh never repented because his heart was hardened by pride. God, however, has a way to humble the proud:

> *Behold, I am against thee, O thou most proud, saith the Lord GOD of hosts: for thy day is come, the time that I will visit thee. And the most proud shall stumble and fall, and none shall raise him up: and I will kindle a fire in his cities, and it shall devour all round about him* (Jeremiah 50:31,32).

Daniel 4:17 pulls back the curtain in heaven and allows us to see an unusual thing: in heaven there is a court known as the court of the "watchers" or the "holy ones." These angels execute the will of God on the earth. The coming judgment on Nebuchadnezzar is said to be "*. . . by the decree of the watchers, and the demand by the word of the holy ones: . . .* " (Daniel 4:17). In verse 24 we see that the decree "*. . . is the decree of the most High, which is come upon my lord the king.*" We know, therefore, that these angelic beings carry out the will of God on the earth regarding nations and kingdoms.

It was the decree of God and the decree of this heavenly court that Nebuchadnezzar was to live as a beast for a period of seven years. The scientific name for this affliction

NOTES

could be either *lycanthropy,* meaning "a delusion in which one imagines oneself to be a wolf or other wild animal," or *zoanthropy,* meaning "a mental disorder in which one believes oneself to be an animal."

God's judgment upon Nebuchadnezzar was not merely punitive—it was not punishment for punishment's sake. Verses 17, 25, 26, and 32 all tell us the great purpose of God behind this strange experience in the life of this heathen king:

> *. . . to the intent that the living may know that the most High ruleth in the kingdom of men, and giveth it to whomsoever he will, and setteth up over it the basest of men* (Daniel 4:17).

> *. . . till thou know that the most High ruleth in the kingdom of men, and giveth it to whomsoever he will* (Daniel 4:25).

> *. . . after that thou shalt have known that the heavens do rule* (Daniel 4:26).

> *. . . til thou know that the most High ruleth in the kingdom of men, and giveth it to whomsoever he will* (Daniel 4:32).

God was after Nebuchadnezzar's heart! *"God so loved the world . . . ."* No one is so high or so great a sinner that God's love can't reach him.

Despite the prediction of gloom contained in the dream, God's longsuffering and mercy can be seen in Daniel's counsel to the king:

> *Wherefore, O king, let my counsel be acceptable unto thee, and break off thy sins by righteousness, and thine iniquities by shewing mercy to the poor; if it may be a lengthening of thy tranquility* (Daniel 4:27).

It wasn't until twelve months later that Nebuchadnezzar's pride level activated God's judgment. The very same hour

40

in which the king boasted of *his* great accomplishments, the decree of the watchers and the holy ones was carried out:

> *The same hour was the thing fulfilled*
> *upon Nebuchadnezzar: and he was driven*
> *from men, and did eat grass as oxen, and*
> *his body was wet with the dew of heaven,*
> *till his hairs were grown like eagles'*
> *feathers, and his nails like birds' claws*
> (Daniel 4:33).

Daniel had promised the king that according to the dream his kingdom would be waiting for him at the end of seven years:

> *And whereas they commanded to leave*
> *the stump of the tree roots; thy kingdom*
> *shall be sure unto thee, after that thou*
> *shalt have known that the heavens do rule*
> (Daniel 4:26).

Nebuchadnezzar's son no doubt ruled in his stead while the king roamed the famous Hanging Gardens munching on grass and leaves! At the end of seven years, however, something wonderful happened:

> *And at the end of the days I Nebuchadnezzar*
> *lifted up mine eyes unto heaven, and*
> *mine understanding returned unto me, and*
> *I blessed the most High, and I praised*
> *and honoured him that liveth for ever,*

41

whose dominion is an everlasting dominion, and his kingdom is from generation to generation: And all the inhabitants of the earth are reputed as nothing: and he doeth according to his will in the army of heaven, and among the inhabitants of the earth: and none can stay his hand, or say unto him, What doest thou? (Daniel 4:34,35).

When King Nebuchadnezzar lifted up his eyes to heaven, his reasoning returned to him:

At the same time my reason returned unto me; and for the glory of my kingdom, mine honour and brightness returned unto me; and my counsellors and my lords sought unto me; and I was established in my kingdom, and excellent majesty was added unto me (Daniel 4:36).

You cannot reason well and be in pride. You cannot think God's thoughts and walk in God's wisdom while your heart is puffed up with pride. Nebuchadnezzar's reasoning returned to him when he started praising and worshiping the most high God.

Finally, we read the lesson that King Nebuchadnezzar learned through God's judgment on his life:

Now I Nebuchadnezzar praise and extol and honour the King of heaven, all whose works are truth, and his ways judgment: and those that walk in pride he is able to abase (Daniel 4:37).

Because four slaves walked in PURPOSE, PRAYER, PERCEPTION, and POWER, the most powerful man on earth bowed before the true God and left a marvelous testimony of his conversion. This is an amazing chapter of history and of victory!

CHAPTER FIVE
A Prophecy Fulfilled

This chapter, chronologically, follows chapters seven and eight. Daniel no doubt put it here so that the visions and prophecies of chapters 7-13 would flow uninterrupted. Let's look at the timing of these sections:

In the first year of Belshazzar king of Babylon Daniel had a dream and visions of his head upon his bed: then he wrote the dream, and told the sum of the matters (Daniel 7:1).

In the third year of the reign of king Belshazzar a vision appeared unto me, even unto me Daniel, after that which appeared unto me at the first (Daniel 8:1).

In the first year of Darius the son of Ahasuerus, of the seed of the Medes, which was made king over the realm of the Chaldeans (Daniel 9:1).

In the third year of Cyrus king of Persia a thing was revealed unto Daniel, whose name was called Belteshazzar; and the thing was true, but the time appointed was long: and he understood the thing, and had understanding of the vision (Daniel 10:1).

Also I in the first year of Darius the Mede, even I, stood to confirm and to strengthen him (Daniel 11:1).

NOTES

Most likely Darius the Mede of chapters 9 and 11 was a general-appointed-ruler under Cyrus the Persian of chapter 10. It was this Cyrus who issued the decree allowing the Jews to return to their homeland. Isaiah had prophesied of him two hundred years before his birth:

> *That saith of Cyrus, He is my shepherd, and shall perform all my pleasure: even saying to Jerusalem, Thou shalt be built; and to the temple, Thy foundation shall be laid* (Isaiah 44:28).

In Daniel chapter five we are given the historical record of the fall of mighty Babylon. According to an ancient historian by the name of Herodotus, Babylon was surrounded by a wall 87 feet thick and 350 feet high. This wall ran almost 15 miles on each side or 60 miles around! There were 250 towers on the walls, and six chariots could drive abreast along the top of the wall.

The city spanned both sides of the Euphrates River. Historians record that there was a palace on each side of the river connected by a subterranean passageway.

Adjacent to the palace was the famous "hanging gardens" of Babylon, one of the seven wonders of the ancient world. Nebuchadnezzar is said to have built these gardens to remind one of his foreign wives of her mountainous homeland. Built in terraces, the gardens rose to a height of 350 feet and covered an area 400 feet square! Isaiah well described Babylon as " . . . *the glory of kingdoms, . . .* ":

> *And Babylon, the glory of kingdoms, the beauty of the Chaldees' excellency, shall be as when God overthrew Sodom and Gomorrah* (Isaiah 13:19).

Jeremiah prophesied of Belshazzar. Speaking of Nebuchadnezzar, he said:

> *And all nations shall serve him, and his son, and his son's son, until the very time of his land come: and then many nations and great kings shall serve themselves of him* (Jeremiah 27:7).

44

While Belshazzar's father, Nabonidus, was away on a military campaign, Belshazzar threw a great feast. Feasts were not uncommon in Babylon, and we recall the banquet given by Queen Esther for the king of her day:

> *And Esther answered, If it seem good unto the king, let the king and Haman come this day unto the banquet that I have prepared for him. Then the king said, Cause Haman to make haste, that he may do as Esther hath said. So the king and Haman came to the banquet that Esther had prepared* (Esther 5:4,5).

Just as Esther's feast turned history for the Jews, Belshazzar's feast would be the turning point in the history of Babylon. Daniel's interpretation of Nebuchadnezzar's image in Daniel chapter 2 was about to be fulfilled:

> *And after thee* [Nebuchadnezzar] *shall arise another kingdom inferior to thee, . . . ''* (Daniel 2:39).

The Babylonian Empire—the head of gold—would now be replaced with the breast and arms of silver. Babylon was in a state of war, and the armies of the Medes and the Persians were encamped outside its walls. Belshazzar trusted in his walls rather than trusting in the living God. Despite his grandfather's conversion and testimony of faith in the true God, Belshazzar chose to worship false deities:

> *They . . . praised the gods of gold, and of silver, of brass, of iron, of wood, and of stone* (Daniel 5:4).

The feast was actually a licentious, drunken, idolatrous brawl. Belshazzar, while under the influence of wine, commanded that the sacred vessels taken out of the Temple in Jerusalem by Nebuchadnezzar 70 years previous be brought into the feast. The sacrilege which resulted filled the cup of Babylon's iniquity, setting the stage for God's hand of judgment:

NOTES

Then they brought the golden vessels that were taken out of the temple of the house of God which was at Jerusalem; and the king, and his princes, his wives, and his concubines, drank in them. They drank wine, and praised the gods of gold, and of silver, of brass, of iron, of wood, and of stone (Daniel 5:3,4).

Alcohol breaks down the human will; the thought to use the sacred vessels of the Jews, which evidently had been stored away for over 70 years, came *after* the king had been drinking wine. You are never safe from temptation while you are consuming alcohol; sipping saints are slipping saints!

God wasted no time in judging this wickedness:

In the same hour came forth fingers of a man's hand, and wrote over against the candlestick upon the plaister of the wall of the king's palace: and the king saw the part of the hand that wrote (Daniel 5:5).

The finger of God wrote upon the wall right above the candlestick where it could be clearly seen by everyone. Belshazzar saw it most clearly, and it set his knees to knocking:

Then the king's countenance was changed, and his thoughts troubled him, so that the

46

joints of his loins were loosed, and his knees smote one against another (Daniel 5:6).

God had predicted just such a reaction from this heathen king two hundred years earlier:

Thus saith the LORD to his anointed, to Cyrus, whose right hand I have holden, to subdue nations before him; and I will loose the loins of kings, . . . (Isaiah 45:1).

The king called in all his "wise men" to interpret the writing. Once again these imposters were at a loss to come up with an answer as to the meaning of the mysterious writing.

The queen (undoubtedly referring to Belshazzar's mother) was called in, and her memory of former days enabled her to make a recommendation to the king which brought Daniel before Belshazzar to interpret the writing:

There is a man in thy kingdom, in whom is the spirit of the holy gods; and in the days of thy father light and understanding and wisdom, like the wisdom of the gods, was found in him; whom the king Nebuchadnezzar thy father, the king, I say, thy father,

47

NOTES

made master of the magicians, astrologers, Chaldeans, and soothsayers; Forasmuch as an excellent spirit, and knowledge, and understanding, interpreting of dreams, and shewing of hard sentences, and dissolving of doubts, were found in the same Daniel, whom the king named Belteshazzar: now let Daniel be called, and he will shew the interpretation (Daniel 5:11,12).

It should be noted that "father" and "grandfather" are both correct translations from the same word; Nebuchadnezzar was Belshazzar's *grand*father, as we have mentioned before.

It had been 65 years since Daniel had interpreted Nebuchadnezzar's dream. If Daniel was 20 years old when taken captive to Babylon, he was now 88 years of age. Belshazzar promised Daniel that he would be the third ruler (after Belshazzar's father and himself) if he could interpret the handwriting—an empty reward seeing that the Babylonian Empire would fall that very night!

Daniel took advantage of the situation to reprove the king in front of his closest friends. Belshazzar knew of the pride that had sent Nebuchadnezzar eating grass and leaves, and he also knew of his grandfather's repentance and conversion. Despite this knowledge, Belshazzar chose to ignore the way of righteousness:

And thou his son, O Belshazzar, hast not humbled thine heart, though thou knewest all this; But hast lifted up thyself against the Lord of heaven; and they have brought the vessels of his house before thee, and thou, and thy lords, thy wives, and thy concubines, have drunk wine in them; and thou hast praised the gods of silver, and gold, of brass, iron, wood, and stone, which see not, nor hear, nor know: and the God in whose hand thy breath is, and whose are all thy ways, hast thou not glorified (Daniel 5:22,23).

48

The finger of God had written, "MENE, MENE, TEKEL, UPHARSIN," and Daniel was given its interpretation:

This is the interpretation of the thing: MENE; God hath numbered thy kingdom, and finished it. TEKEL; Thou art weighed in the balances, and art found wanting. PERES; Thy kingdom is divided, and given to the Medes and Persians (Daniel 5:26-28).

According to his promise, Belshazzar made Daniel the third ruler, but that very night Belshazzar was slain, and Babylon was taken by Cyrus.

The conquest of Babylon was very unique. Herodotus gives us the fascinating details of Babylon's capture:

"Cyrus . . . then advanced against Babylon. But the Babylonians, having taken the field, awaited his coming; and when he had advanced near the city, the Babylonians gave battle, and, being defeated, were shut up in the city. But as they had been long aware of the restless spirit of Cyrus, and saw that he attacked all nations alike, they had laid up provisions for many years, and therefore were under no apprehensions about a siege. On the other hand, Cyrus found himself in difficulty, since much time had elapsed, and his affairs were not at all advanced. Whether, therefore, someone else made the suggestion to him in his perplexity, or whether he himself devised the plan, he had recourse to the following stratagem.

NOTES

"Having stationed the bulk of his army near the passage of the river where it enters Babylon, and again having stationed another division beyond the city, where the river makes its exit, he gave order to his forces to enter the city as soon as they should see the stream fordable. Having stationed his forces and given these directions, he himself marched away with the ineffective part of his army; and having come to the lake, Cyrus did the same with respect to the river and the lake as the queen of the Babylonians had done; for having diverted the river, by means of a canal, into the lake, which was before a swamp, he made the ancient channel fordable by the sinking of the river.

"When this took place, the Persians who were appointed to that purpose close to the stream of the river, which had now subsided to about the middle of a man's thigh, entered Babylon by this passage. If, however, the Babylonians had been aware of it beforehand, or had known what Cyrus was about, they would not have suffered the Persians to enter the city, but would have utterly destroyed them; for, having shut all the little gates that lead to the river, and mounting the walls that extend along the banks of the river, they would have caught them as in a net; whereas the Persians came upon them by surprise.

"It is related by the people who inhabited this city, that, by reason of its great extent, when they who were at the extremities were taken, those of the Babylonians who inhabited the centre knew nothing of the capture (for it happened to be a festival); but they were dancing at the time, and enjoying themselves, till they received certain information of the truth. And thus Babylon was taken for the first time." [1]

God had given a description of this event very clearly through the prophet Isaiah:

> *Thus saith the LORD to his anointed, to Cyrus, whose right hand I have holden, to subdue nations before him; and I will loose the loins of kings, to open before him the two leaved gates; and the gates shall not be shut; I will go before thee, and make the crooked places straight: I will break in pieces the gates of brass,*

---

1. Herodotus, 1:190-91.

50

and cut in sunder the bars of iron: And I will give thee the treasures of darkness, and hidden riches of secret places, that thou mayest know that I, the LORD, which call thee by thy name, am the God of Israel. For Jacob my servant's sake, and Israel mine elect, I have even called thee by thy name: I have surnamed thee, though thou hast not known me (Isaiah 45:1-4).

God described the very gates of Babylon before they were even built! Both Isaiah and Jeremiah had prophesied that Babylon would fall in the exact manner described by Daniel:

Behold, I will stir up the Medes against them, which shall not regard silver; and as for gold, they shall not delight in it (Isaiah 13:17).

. . . Go up, O Elam: besiege, O Media; . . . Therefore are my loins filled with pain: pangs have taken hold upon me, as the pangs of a woman that travaileth: I was bowed down at the hearing of it; I was dismayed at the seeing of it. My heart panted, fearfulness affrighted me: the night of my pleasure hath he turned into fear unto me. Prepare the table, watch in the watchtower, eat, drink: arise, ye princes, and anoint the shield (Isaiah 21:2-5).

For thus saith the LORD of hosts, the God of Israel; The daughter of Babylon is like a threshingfloor, it is time to thresh her: yet a little while, and the time of her harvest shall come. Therefore thus saith the LORD; Behold, I will plead thy cause, and take vengeance for thee; and I will dry up her sea, and make her springs dry (Jeremiah 51:33,36).

NOTES

NOTES

Many of these prophecies have their ultimate fulfillment upon the commercial and religious Babylon described in Revelation 17 and 18:

> *And he cried mightily with a strong voice, saying, Babylon the great is fallen, is fallen, and is become the habitation of devils, and the hold of every foul spirit, and a cage of every unclean and hateful bird. And I heard another voice from heaven, saying, Come out of her, my people, that ye be not partakers of her sins, and that ye receive not of her plagues* (Revelation 18:2,4).

(Bibliography:)

Herodotus. Vol. 1. Trans. Henry Carey. New York: Harper, 1889.

CHAPTER SIX
Preparation for Crises

We come now to a story known by every child who has ever attended Sunday school—Daniel in the lions' den. In a book of 13 chapters, with astounding visions and prophecies of future events, it is of more than passing interest that God would devote 28 verses relating this particular incident in the life of Daniel. Clearly, God desires that we pay close attention to the lessons contained in this sixth chapter! End-time prophecy is exciting, and God wishes for us to know *future* events; however, we still need a practical, working faith to cause us to always triumph in Christ in the *present*.

Babylon had been overthrown and divided between the Medes and the Persians. It was now time for Darius to organize the kingdom for purposes of control and taxation. All of this background information allows us to see the place of highest honor accorded to Daniel within the political structure of his day:

> *It pleased Darius to set over the kingdom an hundred and twenty princes, which should be over the whole kingdom; And over these three presidents; of whom Daniel was first: that the princes might give accounts unto them, and the king should have no damage* (Daniel 6:1,2).

There were 120 princes who were set over the provinces of Darius' kingdom. Daniel was one of three "presidents" chosen to rule over the princes. There is no limit to what God can do in promoting the person who relies solely on Him—Daniel was even preferred above the other two presidents:

> *Then this Daniel was preferred above the*

NOTES

NOTES

presidents and princes, because an excellent spirit was in him; and the king thought to set him over the whole realm (Daniel 6:3).

Notice that "because" in verse three. Daniel wasn't preferred above the other presidents because of his good looks, or because of his ancestry, or because of his contacts within the king's court, or for any other reason. Daniel was preferred **because** his first priority was his relationship with the Spirit of God:

But seek ye first the kingdom of God, and his righteousness; and all these things shall be added unto you (Matthew 6:33).

Daniel's place of authority and power was one of the *all things* promised to anyone who will seek first God's interests on the earth.

The fact that a 90-year-old Jewish eunuch and former slave enjoyed such high favor with the king, plus Daniel's honesty and integrity, which would have precluded any corruption among the other officials, served to bring the younger officials' jealousy out into the open:

Then the presidents and princes sought to find occasion against Daniel concerning the kingdom; but they could find none occasion nor fault; forasmuch as he was faithful, neither was there any error or fault found in him. Then said these men,

54

We shall not find any occasion against
this Daniel, except we find it against him
concerning the law of his God (Daniel 6:4,5).

A diabolical plot was hatched to remove Daniel from his
position of honor. But what a testimony Daniel had—with
his enemies, no less! The life we live before our relatives
and neighbors speaks loud indeed. The gospel is not
always preached from the pulpit or in special crusades.
Most of the time the gospel is seen in the routine things
we do every day—a kind word, a smile, or an offer to
pray for someone's need. This kind of "preaching" leads
eventually to an openness on behalf of unbelievers to hear
the plan of salvation shared in a clear way.

The officials finally came up with a plan to trap Daniel.
Through flattering the king they were able to have Darius
pass a decree prohibiting prayer to anyone but himself for
30 days:

> *Then these presidents and princes*
> *assembled together to the king, and said*
> *thus unto him, King Darius, live for ever.*
> *All the presidents of the kingdom, the*
> *governors, and the princes, the counsellors,*
> *and the captains, have consulted together*
> *to establish a royal statute, and to make*
> *a firm decree, that whosoever shall ask a*
> *petition of any God or man for thirty*
> *days, save of thee, O king, he shall be*
> *cast into the den of lions* (Daniel 6:6,7).

Daniel was undaunted by the new law. Despite knowing
that the penalty for defying the king's decree was to be
cast into a pit of hungry lions, Daniel remained steadfast
in PURPOSE and in PRAYER. He was prepared for any crisis:

> *Now when Daniel knew that the writing*
> *was signed, he went into his house; and*
> *his windows being open in his chamber*
> *toward Jerusalem, he kneeled upon his*
> *knees three times a day, and prayed, and*
> *gave thanks before his God, as he did*
> *aforetime* (Daniel 6:10).

NOTES

Solomon had begun the practice of praying toward Jerusalem:

If thy people go out to war against their enemies by the way that thou shalt send them, and they pray unto thee toward this city which thou hast chosen, and the house which I have built for thy name; Then hear thou from the heavens their prayer and their supplication, and maintain their cause (II Chronicles 6:34,35).

King David prayed three times each day:

As for me, I will call upon God; and the LORD shall save me. Evening, and morning, and at noon, will I pray, and cry aloud: and he shall hear my voice (Psalms 55:16,17).

According to Daniel 9:2, Daniel had the book of Jeremiah before him with its instructions to the exiles in Babylon concerning prayer:

Thus saith the LORD of hosts, the God of Israel, unto all that are carried away captives, whom I have caused to be carried away from Jerusalem unto Babylon; Then shall ye call upon me, and ye shall go and pray unto me, and I will hearken unto you. And ye shall seek me, and find me, when ye shall search for me with all your heart (Jeremiah 29:4,12,13).

Daniel's enemies knew that he would not be unfaithful to his God, therefore they waited to catch him violating the king's decree. They lost no time in reporting Daniel's behavior to Darius:

Then these men assembled, and found Daniel praying and making supplication before his God. Then they came near, and spake before the king concerning the king's decree; Hast thou not signed a decree, that every man that shall ask a

56

petition of any God or man within thirty days, save of thee, O king, shall be cast into the den of lions? The king answered and said, The thing is true, according to the law of the Medes and Persians, which altereth not. Then answered they and said before the king, That Daniel, which is of the children of the captivity of Judah, regardeth not thee, O king, nor the decree that thou hast signed, but maketh his petition three times a day (Daniel 6:11-13).

The king was helpless to change his decree. It was the Persian belief that the king was the representative of their gods. Having once decreed the law, Darius was obligated to carry it out. The king saw how foolishly he had behaved, however, and he was mortified at the inevitable consequences of his actions: Daniel must be cast into the lions' den:

Then the king commanded, and they brought Daniel, and cast him into the den of lions. . . . (Daniel 6:16).

Notice the confession of King Darius to Daniel:

. . . Now the king spake and said unto Daniel, Thy God whom thou servest continually, he will deliver thee (Daniel 6:16).

57

NOTES

From what we read in verse 20, it is doubtful that the king was speaking from any real conviction of faith in Daniel's God—at least not yet:

> *Then the king arose very early in the morning, and went in haste unto the den of lions. And when he came to the den, he cried with a lamentable voice unto Daniel: and the king spake and said to Daniel, O Daniel, servant of the living God, is thy God, whom thou servest continually, able to deliver thee from the lions?* (Daniel 6:19,20).

Such was Daniel's favor with the king that Darius fasted, went without his usual entertainment, and stayed up all night in agitation over Daniel's fate.

The king was powerless—but the King of kings was not! Darius would witness the power of the living God as he peered into the shadowy lion pit and heard the voice of Daniel:

> *Then said Daniel unto the king, O king, live for ever. My God hath sent his angel, and hath shut the lions' mouths, that they have not hurt me: forasmuch as before him innocency was found in me; and also before thee, O king, have I done no hurt* (Daniel 6:21,22).

Daniel attributed his deliverance to his innocence before God and man. The king ordered Daniel to be taken out of the pit, and we read of another cause for this miraculous display of God's power:

> *Then was the king exceeding glad for him, and commanded that they should take Daniel up out of the den. So Daniel was taken up out of the den, and no manner of hurt was found upon him, because he believed in his God* (Daniel 6:23).

With this the New Testament writer to the Hebrews agrees:

Who through faith subdued kingdoms,
wrought righteousness, obtained promises,
stopped the mouths of lions (Hebrews 11:33).

Daniel's faith was vindicated. However, Daniel's deliverance did not satisfy the king. Unhappy that he had been manipulated, King Darius ordered those officials who had accused Daniel to be thrown into the lion's den along with their families.

Were the lions simply not hungry while Daniel was in their midst? Verse 24 removes all doubts that it was Daniel's God Who saved His prophet:

And the king commanded, and they
brought those men which had accused
Daniel, and they cast them into the den
of lions, them, their children, and their
wives; and the lions had the mastery of
them, and brake all their bones in pieces
or ever they came at the bottom of the
den (Daniel 6:24).

God finally got King Darius' attention. The "signs" which followed Daniel the believer (Mark 16:17,18) brought about the conversion of the second gentile world ruler. Like Nebuchadnezzar, Darius issued a written testimony of his faith in the true God:

Then king Darius wrote unto all people,
nations, and languages, that dwell in all
the earth; Peace be multiplied unto you. I
make a decree, That in every dominion of
my kingdom men tremble and fear before
the God of Daniel: for he is the living
God, and stedfast for ever, and his
kingdom that which shall not be
destroyed, and his dominion shall be even
unto the end. He delivereth and rescueth,
and he worketh signs and wonders in
heaven and in earth, who hath delivered

NOTES

Daniel from the power of the lions (Daniel 6:25-27).

Don't ever think that YOU can't change a city, a nation, or the world. If a lowly eunuch slave can rise to the top of two heathen empires and pray in the conversion of the two most powerful men in their day, so can YOU! Don't ever think or say you are too insignificant.

PURPOSE in your heart to be committed to God, and PRAY the Word over your household, your city, and your nation. God will get through to world leaders if we will do our part—if we will PURPOSE and PRAY.

Look at the last verse of chapter 6—no one can be a person of prayer and not prosper:

So this Daniel prospered in the reign of Darius, and in the reign of Cyrus the Persian (Daniel 6:28).

There is no question that God wants His people to have soul prosperity—success in all aspects of life. Daniel chapter six was written so that you and I could learn the key to being successful in every area of life—every day!

CHAPTER SEVEN
World History in Three Visions

We come now to a more intensely prophetic part of the book of Daniel. The first six chapters dealt with mostly historical information, while the last six chapters deal primarily with great prophetic themes. God writes history centuries before it comes to pass so that His people will be prepared.

God's Word is profitable in every age, but there is a specific time when revelation or prophecy within His Word is to be literally fulfilled. At that proper time the prophecy will be completely understood.

This is the chapter of world history, similar to chapter two, as seen through Daniel's three visions:

(1) the vision of the four wild animals (verses 1-8),

(2) the vision of God's judgment (verses 9-12), and

(3) the vision of the Son of Man receiving His kingdom (verses 13,14).

This was the first time Daniel received a dream or vision *directly* from God. Remember, you must first sow into others' dreams before you can reap your own dreams!

In chapter four of Daniel we saw that without God's presence and God's care, man is no better off than the beast of the field. Daniel saw this truth literally fulfilled in Nebuchadnezzar's life. Now, Daniel is about to receive a vision similar to Nebuchadnezzar's dream of the metallic image—only this time, instead of the great world empires being represented by an image of gold, silver, brass, and iron, Daniel sees these world empires as beasts—in contrast to God's kingdom which is set up by the Son of Man.

NOTES

VISION ONE
Daniel 7:1-8

In the first year of Belshazzar king of Babylon Daniel had a dream and visions of his head upon his bed: then he wrote the dream, and told the sum of the matters (Daniel 7:1).

Notice that we are back in the first year of King Belshazzar. This vision occurred before the fall of Babylon and belongs before chapter five *chronologically.* Daniel's first vision begins with four winds agitating the sea:

Daniel spake and said, I saw in my vision by night, and, behold, the four winds of the heaven strove upon the great sea (Daniel 7:2).

Winds represent war, strife, and judgment—all occurring in the area currently controlled by Satan:

Wherein in time past ye walked according to the course of this world, according to the prince of the power of the air, the spirit that now worketh in the children of disobedience (Ephesians 2:2).

For we wrestle not against flesh and blood, but against principalities, against powers, against the rulers of the darkness of this world, against spiritual wickedness in high places (Ephesians 6:12).

And after these things I saw four angels standing on the four corners of the earth, holding the four winds of the earth, that the wind should not blow on the earth, nor on the sea, nor on any tree. And I saw another angel ascending from the east, having the seal of the living God: and he cried with a loud voice to the four angels, to whom it was given to hurt the earth and the sea (Revelation 7:1,2).

And, behold, there came a great wind from the wilderness, and smote the four corners of the house, and it fell upon the young men, and they are dead; . . . (Job 1:19).

Thus saith the LORD of hosts, Behold, evil shall go forth from nation to nation, and a great whirlwind shall be raised up from the coasts of the earth (Jeremiah 25:32).

The "great sea" that Daniel mentions represents nations and peoples:

Forasmuch as this people refuseth the waters of Shiloah that go softly, and rejoice in Rezin and Remaliah's son; Now therefore, behold, the Lord bringeth up upon them the waters of the river, strong and many, even the king of Assyria, and all his glory: and he shall come up over all his channels, and go over all his banks (Isaiah 8:6,7).

Woe to the multitude of many people, which make a noise like the noise of the seas; and to the rushing of nations, that make a rushing like the rushing of mighty waters! The nations shall rush like the rushing of many waters: but God shall rebuke them, and they shall flee far off, and shall be chased as the chaff of the mountains before the wind, and like a rolling thing before the whirlwind (Isaiah 17:12,13).

Again, the kingdom of heaven is like unto a net, that was cast into the sea, and gathered of every kind: . . . (Matthew 13:47).

And he saith unto me, The waters which thou sawest, where the whore sitteth, are peoples, and multitudes, and nations, and tongues (Revelation 17:15).

NOTES

Out of this "great sea" Daniel saw four beasts arise:

And four great beasts came up from the sea, diverse one from another (Daniel 7:3).

Daniel is not left guessing as to what these four beasts represent:

These great beasts, which are four, are four kings, which shall arise out of the earth (Daniel 7:17).

God sees these four kingdoms as wild beasts, devouring one another. Each one takes his supremacy by brute force: while the lion devours, the bear is crushing. The leopard is quick and agile, drawing blood from his victim. The fourth beast, as we shall see, is unlike any of the others.

It is not unusual, even in our day, for nations to have animals as national emblems: Great Britain has a lion as its emblem, America has the eagle, China is symbolized as a dragon, and Russia is seen as a bear.

The First Beast—Babylon

The first was like a lion, and had eagle's wings: I beheld till the wings thereof were plucked, and it was lifted up from the earth, and made stand upon the feet as a man, and a man's heart was given to it (Daniel 7:4).

Lions and eagles are symbolic of royalty in the Bible:

And there were six steps to the throne, with a footstool of gold, which were fastened to the throne, and stays on each side of the sitting place, and two lions standing by the stays: And twelve lions stood there on the one side and on the other upon the six steps. There was not the like made in any kingdom (II Chronicles 9:18,19).

And say, Thus saith the Lord GOD; A great eagle with great wings, longwinged, full of feathers, which had divers colours, came unto Lebanon, and took the highest branch of the cedar (Ezekiel 17:3).

The lion is the king of the beasts, just as Babylon was the head of gold in Nebuchadnezzar's dream. This beast had the wings of an eagle, the king of the birds. Nebuchadnezzar had swiftly conquered all civilized nations, but Daniel watched as the wings were plucked—exactly what happened to Nebuchadnezzar in losing his kingdom for a time (Daniel 4). In Daniel 4:32 we saw how Nebuchadnezzar lifted up his eyes, received his understanding back, and was given a new heart!

The Second Beast— Medo-Persia

NOTES

And behold another beast, a second, like to a bear, and it raised up itself on one side, and it had three ribs in the mouth of it between the teeth of it: and they said thus unto it, Arise, devour much flesh (Daniel 7:5).

The bear is considered the strongest animal after the lion. It is not as agile as the lion, but awkward with brute force and great strength:

And he turned back, and looked on them, and cursed them in the name of the LORD. And there came forth two she bears out of the wood, and tare forty and two children of them (II Kings 2:24).

Behold, I will stir up the Medes against them, which shall not regard silver; and as for gold, they shall not delight in it. Their bows also shall dash the young men to pieces; and they shall have no pity on the fruit of the womb; their eye shall not spare children (Isaiah 13:17,18).

The bear is certainly a good representation of the Medo-Persian Empire. It got up on one side and then the other—a picture of the two-sided empire of the Medes and the Persians. The three ribs in the bear's mouth represent the Medo-Persian conquests of Babylon, Lydia, and Egypt. The bear went on to "devour much flesh"—it conquered much more territory before its eventual downfall.

The bear corresponds to the silver breast and arms of Nebuchadnezzar's image in Daniel chapter two.

The Third Beast—Greece

After this I beheld, and lo another, like a leopard, which had upon the back of it four wings of a fowl; the beast had also four heads; and dominion was given to it (Daniel 7:6).

This beast is unusual in that it has *four* wings and *four* heads. A leopard is very strong and very quick:

Their horses also are swifter than the leopards, and are more fierce than the evening wolves: . . . (Habakkuk 1:8).

The speed of this animal, represented by the four wings, is characteristic of the tremendous conquests of Alexander the Great as he subdued the Medo-Persian Empire and conquered the whole civilized world in a very short time. The four heads of this beast represent the four divisions of Alexander's kingdom after his death: Thrace (Turkey), Syria, Egypt, and Macedonia.

The leopard corresponds to the abdomen of brass of Nebuchadnezzar's image.

The Fourth Beast—Rome

After this I saw in the night visions, and behold a fourth beast, dreadful and terrible, and strong exceedingly; and it had great iron teeth: it devoured and brake in pieces, and stamped the residue with the feet of it: and it was diverse from all the beasts that were before it; and it had ten horns (Daniel 7:7).

This fourth beast was hideous to look at. It had iron teeth and ten horns, which, of course, correspond to the iron legs and the ten toes of Nebuchadnezzar's great image. Rome ruled the world with an iron hand and certainly broke in pieces anyone who came against it. The Jews who found themselves trapped in the siege of Jerusalem in 70 A.D. learned of Rome's "dreadful and terrible" power.

This beast with ten horns is similar to the beast with ten horns found in the last book of the Bible:

So he carried me away in the spirit into the wilderness: and I saw a woman sit upon a scarlet coloured beast, full of names of blasphemy, having seven heads and ten horns. And the ten horns which thou sawest are ten kings, which have received no kingdom as yet; but receive power as kings one hour with the beast (Revelation 17:3,12).

These horns represent the ten kingdoms with which the Antichrist will be involved. Daniel 7:8 introduces us to the Antichrist:

I considered the horns, and, behold, there came up among them another little horn, before whom there were three of the first horns plucked up by the roots: and, behold, in this horn were eyes like the eyes of man, and a mouth speaking great things (Daniel 7:8).

The fact that this horn has the "eyes of man" and a "mouth speaking great things" tells us that the Antichrist will have unusual perception and be very persuasive.

68

Let's take a closer look at the Antichrist. We learn about him throughout the Old and New Testaments:

Daniel calls him the "little horn" and a "horn":

I considered the horns, and, behold, there came up among them another little horn, before whom there were three of the first horns plucked up by the roots: and, behold, in this horn were eyes like the eyes of man, and a mouth speaking great things (Daniel 7:8).

And of the ten horns that were in his head, and of the other which came up, and before whom three fell: even of that horn that had eyes, and a mouth that spake very great things, whose look was more stout than his fellows. I beheld, and the same horn made war with the saints, and prevailed against them (Daniel 7:20,21).

And the ten horns out of this kingdom are ten kings that shall arise: and another shall rise after them; and he shall be diverse from the first, and he shall subdue three kings. And he shall speak great words against the most High, and shall wear out the saints of the most High, and think to change times and laws: and they shall be given into his hand until a time and times and the dividing of time (Daniel 7:24,25).

Compare these descriptions of the Antichrist in Daniel with John's description of him in Revelation:

And there was given unto him a mouth speaking great things and blasphemies; and power was given unto him to continue forty and two months. And he opened his mouth in blasphemy against God, to

69

NOTES

blaspheme his name, and his tabernacle, and them that dwell in heaven. And it was given unto him to make war with the saints, and to overcome them: and power was given him over all kindreds, and tongues, and nations (Revelation 13:5-7).

Daniel makes mention of him as the "king of fierce countenance":

And in the latter time of their kingdom, when the transgressors are come to the full, a king of fierce countenance, and understanding dark sentences, shall stand up (Daniel 8:23).

The Antichrist is referred to as "the prince that shall come":

And after threescore and two weeks shall Messiah be cut off, but not for himself: and the people of the prince that shall come shall destroy the city and the sanctuary; and the end thereof shall be with a flood, and unto the end of the war desolations are determined (Daniel 9:26).

Daniel also describes the Antichrist as a "vile person":

And in his estate shall stand up a vile person, to whom they shall not give the honour of the kingdom: but he shall come in peaceably, and obtain the kingdom by flatteries (Daniel 11:21).

Lastly, Daniel calls the Antichrist a willful king:

And the king shall do according to his will; and he shall exalt himself, and magnify himself above every god, and shall speak marvellous things against the God of gods, and shall prosper till the indignation be accomplished: for that that is determined shall be done (Daniel 11:36).

70

Isaiah calls the Antichrist the "Assyrian":

O Assyrian, the rod of mine anger, and
the staff in their hand is mine indignation
(Isaiah 10:5).

The LORD of hosts hath sworn, saying,
Surely as I have thought, so shall it come
to pass; and as I have purposed, so shall
it stand: That I will break the Assyrian in
my land, and upon my mountains tread
him under foot: then shall his yoke depart
from off them, and his burden depart
from off their shoulders (Isaiah 14:24,25).

For through the voice of the LORD shall
the Assyrian be beaten down, which
smote with a rod (Isaiah 30:31).

The Antichrist is called "the wicked":

But with righteousness shall he judge the
poor, and reprove with equity for the
meek of the earth: and he shall smite the
earth with the rod of his mouth, and with
the breath of his lips shall he slay the wicked
(Isaiah 11:4).

He is called the "king of Babylon":

That thou shalt take up this proverb
against the king of Babylon, and say,
How hath the oppressor ceased! the
golden city ceased! (Isaiah 14:4).

In Judges 9:7-15 we read of a prophetic parable which
shows how the Jews will refuse the truth and accept the
Antichrist to rule over them.

In the New Testament the Antichrist is called the "man
of sin":

Let no man deceive you by any means:
for that day shall not come, except there

71

NOTES

come a falling away first, and that man of sin be revealed, the son of perdition; Who opposeth and exalteth himself above all that is called God, or that is worshipped; so that he as God sitteth in the temple of God, shewing himself that he is God. Remember ye not, that, when I was yet with you, I told you these things?

And now ye know what withholdeth that he might be revealed in his time. For the mystery of iniquity doth already work: only he who now letteth will let, until he be taken out of the way. And then shall that Wicked be revealed, whom the Lord shall consume with the spirit of his mouth, and shall destroy with the brightness of his coming: Even him, whose coming is after the working of Satan with all power and signs and lying wonders (II Thessalonians 2:3-9).

And, of course, he is simply called the "antichrist":

Who is a liar but he that denieth that Jesus is the Christ? He is antichrist, that denieth the Father and the Son (I John 2:22).

Jesus spoke of the Antichrist:

Then if any man shall say unto you, Lo, here is Christ, or, there; believe it not. For there shall arise false Christs, and false prophets, and shall shew great signs and wonders; insomuch that, if it were possible, they shall deceive the very elect (Matthew 24:23,24).

Chapter eight of Daniel will tell us more about the activities of the Antichrist. Some have thought that Judas and the Antichrist are the same: Judas was called the "son of perdition," and the Antichrist is said to "go into perdition":

*While I was with them in the world, I
kept them in thy name: those that thou
gavest me I have kept, and none of them
is lost, but the son of perdition; that the
scripture might be fulfilled* (John 17:12).

*The beast that thou sawest was, and is
not; and shall ascend out of the bottomless
pit, and go into perdition: and they that
dwell on the earth shall wonder, . . .*
(Revelation 17:8).

Judas "was, and is not," indicating that he was on the
earth once, died, and may ascend out of the bottomless pit.

VISION TWO
Daniel 7:9-12

Daniel's second and third visions show us the outcome
of history: judgment upon the nations and the establishment
of Christ's kingdom. Daniel is receiving a step-by-step program
of end-time events which coincides with Revelation 5-22.
In Daniel's second vision we see God's judgment upon the
gentiles and upon the Antichrist:

*I beheld till the thrones were cast down,
and the Ancient of days did sit, whose
garment was white as snow, and the hair
of his head like the pure wool: his throne
was like the fiery flame, and his wheels
as burning fire. A fiery stream issued and*

NOTES

came forth from before him: thousand
thousands ministered unto him, and ten
thousand times ten thousand stood before
him: the judgment was set, and the books
were opened (Daniel 7:9,10).

The "Ancient of days" is no doubt the Father. We
would expect the Son to be like His Father, and that is
what we see in the book of Revelation:

*And in the midst of the seven candlesticks
one like unto the Son of man, clothed
with a garment down to the foot, and girt
about the paps with a golden girdle. His
head and his hairs were white like wool,
as white as snow; and his eyes were as a
flame of fire; And his feet like unto fine
brass, as if they burned in a furnace; and
his voice as the sound of many waters*
(Revelation 1:13-15).

Thrones being "cast down" speaks of principalities and
powers being cast out of heaven:

*And there was war in heaven: Michael
and his angels fought against the dragon;
and the dragon fought and his angels,
And prevailed not; neither was their place
found any more in heaven. And the great
dragon was cast out, that old serpent,
called the Devil, and Satan, which
deceiveth the whole world: he was cast
out into the earth, and his angels were
cast out with him* (Revelation 12:7-9).

At the time of the Rapture of the overcoming Church,
the arrival of millions of Christians in heaven spells the
downfall of Satan. The resulting expulsion of Satan from
heaven to the earth will bring great persecution by the
Antichrist on the people who are saved during the
Tribulation:

*And he shall speak great words against
the most High, and shall wear out the*

*saints of the most High, and think to
change times and laws: and they shall be
given into his hand until a time and times
and the dividing of time* (Daniel 7:25).

During this time there will be great judgments upon the
earth and eventually upon Antichrist, the false prophet,
and Satan:

*I beheld then because of the voice of the
great words which the horn spake; I
beheld even till the beast was slain, and
his body destroyed, and given to the burning
flame* (Daniel 7:11).

*And the beast was taken, and with him
the false prophet that wrought miracles
before him, with which he deceived them
that had received the mark of the beast,
and them that worshipped his image. These
both were cast alive into a lake of fire
burning with brimstone* (Revelation 19:20).

*And the devil that deceived them was cast
into the lake of fire and brimstone, where
the beast and the false prophet are, and
shall be tormented day and night for ever
and ever* (Revelation 20:10).

Daniel witnessed the judgment of the nations. There
are seven basic judgments in the Bible:

(1) The judgment of rebellious angels:

*For if God spared not the angels
that sinned, but cast them down to
hell, and delivered them into chains
of darkness to be reserved unto
judgment* (II Peter 2:4).

(2) The judgment of rebellious Israel:

NOTES

NOTES

And I will cause you to pass under the rod, and I will bring you into the bond of the covenant (Ezekiel 20:37).

(3) The judgment of believers' sins at the Cross:

Now is the judgment of this world; now shall the prince of this world be cast out (John 12:31).

(4) The Christians' self-judgment:

For if we would judge ourselves, we should not be judged. But when we are judged, we are chastened of the Lord, that we should not be condemned with the world (I Corinthians 11:31,32).

(5) The judgment of believers' works:

For we must all appear before the judgment seat of Christ; that every one may receive the things done in his body, according to that he hath done, whether it be good or bad (II Corinthians 5:10).

For other foundation can no man lay than that is laid, which is Jesus Christ. Now if any man build upon this foundation of gold, silver, precious stones, wood, hay, stubble; Every man's work shall declare it, because it shall be revealed by fire; and the fire shall try every man's work of what sort it is. If any man's work abide which he hath build thereupon, he shall receive a reward. If any man's work shall be burned, he shall suffer loss; but he himself

shall be saved; yet so as by fire
(I Corinthians 3:11-15).

(6) The judgment of the nations at the Second Coming:

And before him shall be gathered all
nations; and he shall separate them
one from another; as a shepherd
divideth his sheep from the goats
(Matthew 25:32).

For; behold, in those days, and in
that time, when I shall bring again
the captivity of Judah and Jerusalem,
I will also gather all nations, and
will bring them down into the valley
of Jehoshaphat, and will plead with
them there for my people and for
my heritage Israel, whom they have
scattered among the nations, and
parted my land (Joel 3:1,2).

(7) The judgment of the wicked dead:

And I saw the dead, small and
great, stand before God; and the
books were opened; and another
book was opened, which is the book
of life; and the dead were judged
out of those things which were
written in the books, according to
their works (Revelation 20:12).

Daniel 7:12 tells us that the dominion of the lion, the bear, and the leopard will be taken away:

As concerning the rest of the beasts,
they had their dominion taken
away: yet their lives were prolonged
for a season and time (Daniel 7:12).

NOTES

These "beasts" are, of course, Babylon, Persia, and Greece. Though these empires will be restored in the future and their boundaries will overlap, they will fall again. They will have their "comeback," but they will also have their "fall back."

VISION THREE
Daniel 7:13,14

In the third vision we see the Son of Man receiving His kingdom:

> *I saw in the night visions, and, behold, one like the Son of man came with the clouds of heaven, and came to the Ancient of days, and they brought him near before him. And there was given him dominion, and glory, and a kingdom, that all people, nations, and languages, should serve him: his dominion is an everlasting dominion, which shall not pass away, and his kingdom that which shall not be destroyed (Daniel 7:13,14).*

Jesus is the Son of Man:

> *And Jesus saith unto him, The foxes have holes, and the birds of the air have nests;*

78

but the Son of man hath not where to lay his head (Matthew 8:20).

But that ye may know that the Son of man hath power on earth to forgive sins, (then saith he to the sick of the palsy,) Arise, take up thy bed, and go unto thine house (Matthew 9:6).

But when they persecute you in this city, flee ye into another: for verily I say unto you, Ye shall not have gone over the cities of Israel, till the Son of man be come (Matthew 10:23).

Clouds represent deity:

And the LORD went before them by day in a pillar of a cloud, to lead them the way; and by night in a pillar of fire, to give them light; to go by day and night: He took not away the pillar of the cloud by day, nor the pillar of fire by night, from before the people (Exodus 13:21,22).

And the LORD said unto Moses, Lo, I come unto thee in a thick cloud, that the people may hear when I speak with thee, and believe thee for ever. And Moses told the words of the people unto the LORD (Exodus 19:9).

And it came to pass, when the priests were come out of the holy place, that the cloud filled the house of the LORD, So that the priests could not stand to minister because of the cloud: for the glory of the LORD had filled the house of the LORD (I Kings 8:10,11).

The burden of Egypt. Behold, the LORD rideth upon a swift cloud, and shall come into Egypt: and the idols of Egypt shall

79

NOTES

be moved at his presence, and the heart of Egypt shall melt in the midst of it (Isaiah 19:1).

Then the glory of the LORD went up from the cherub, and stood over the threshold of the house; and the house was filled with the cloud, and the court was full of the brightness of the LORD'S glory (Ezekiel 10:4).

Daniel's vision of the Son of Man returning with clouds was predicted by "two men" in the New Testament:

And when he had spoken these things, while they beheld, he was taken up; and a cloud received him out of their sight. And while they looked stedfastly toward heaven as he went up, behold, two men stood by them in white apparel; Which also said, Ye men of Galilee, why stand ye gazing up into heaven? this same Jesus, which is taken up from you into heaven, shall so come in like manner as ye have seen him go into heaven (Acts 1:9-11).

The disciple John saw this same vision:

Behold, he cometh with clouds; and every eye shall see him, and they also which pierced him: and all kindreds of the earth shall wail because of him. Even so, Amen (Revelation 1:7).

Daniel was greatly troubled by these tremendous visions:

I Daniel was grieved in my spirit in the midst of my body, and the visions of my head troubled me (Daniel 7:15).

Daniel was helped by an angelic interpreter. This is not unusual, for we see it again in the book of Zechariah. The angel tells Daniel that the saints will receive their kingdom:

But the saints of the most High shall take the kingdom, and possess the kingdom for ever, even for ever and ever (Daniel 7:18).

And the kingdom and dominion, and the greatness of the kingdom under the whole heaven, shall be given to the people of the saints of the most High, whose kingdom is an everlasting kingdom, and all dominions shall serve and obey him (Daniel 7:27).

It will be an everlasting and ever expanding kingdom:

Of the increase of his government and peace there shall be no end, upon the throne of David, and upon his kingdom, to order it, and to establish it with judgment and with justice from henceforth even for ever. The zeal of the LORD of hosts will perform this (Isaiah 9:7).

We will be joint heirs with Christ, and we will rule and reign with Him:

And if children, then heirs; heirs of God, and joint-heirs with Christ; if so be that we suffer with him, that we may be also glorified together (Romans 8:17).

And he that overcometh, and keepeth my works unto the end, to him will I give power over the nations: And he shall rule them with a rod of iron; as the vessels of a potter shall they be broken to shivers: even as I received of my Father (Revelation 2:26,27).

NOTES

81

HARMONY OF DANIEL'S EMPIRE VISIONS

	Chapter 2	Chapter 7	Chapter 8	Chapter 11	Revelation	Olivet Discourse — Others
1st Empire Babylonian	Head of Gold Dan. 2:31, 32, 37, 38	LION Dan. 7:1-4			Mouth as the mouth of a lion Rev. 13:2	
2nd Empire Medo-Persian	Arms of Silver Dan. 2:32, 39	BEAR Two Sides Dan. 7:5	RAM Two Horns Dan. 8:3, 20	KINGS OF PERSIA Dan. 11:2	Feet as the feet of a bear Rev. 13:2	
3rd Empire Grecian	Trunk of Brass Dan. 2:32, 39	LEOPARD Four Heads Dan. 7:6	GOAT Four Horns Dan. 8:5, 8, 21	A MIGHTY KING Dan. 11:3, 4	Like unto a leopard Rev. 13:2	
4th Empire Roman	Legs of Iron Dan. 2:33, 40	BEAST Dan. 7:7		INTERVENING WARS KING OF THE NORTH Dan. 11:15-19	Beast out of the sea Rev. 13:1	
Divided Empire	Ten Toes Iron and Clay Dan. 2:33, 41	TEN HORNS Dan. 7:7	In the latter time of their kingdom; when the transgressors are come to the full Dan. 8:23	Fall of the Roman Empire Dan. 11:19	Seven heads and ten horns Crowns on his horns Rev. 13:1	
Rise of Antichrist		LITTLE HORN Out of the head of the beast Mouth speaking great things Subdue three kings Dan. 7:8	LITTLE HORN Out of one of the four winds Waxes great Destroy wonderful things * * * * Peace and Craft Dan. 8:9, 18-25	RAISER OF TAXES In the glory of the kingdom Dan. 11:20	Dragon gave him his throne Rev. 13:2 Mouth speaking great things Rev. 13:5	Wars and Commotions Matt. 24:6; Luke 21:9 Peace and Safety I Thess. 5:3
Rapture Revelation of the Man of sin		THRONES CAST DOWN Judgment Throne set up Action starts in Heaven Books opened Dan. 7:9-14	STARS CAST DOWN Dan. 8:10-12	Antichrist killed: neither in anger nor in battle Dan. 11:20 SATAN REVEALED A Vile Person Dan. 11:21, 22	Man child caught up to heaven War in heaven Satan cast down to the earth Rev. 12:5, 7-10 Head wounded and healed Rev. 13:3	As in the days of Noah One taken, another left Matt. 24:37-41 Escape from a time of trouble Dan. 12:1; Isa. 26:19-21 Zeph. 2:3
Tribulation Day of the Lord		TRIBULATION SAINTS Dan. 7:24, 25	DESTROY HOLY PEOPLE Abomination of Desolation Dan. 8:12-14, 24	WARS OF ANTICHRIST Dan. 11:23-43	Opens his mouth in blasphemy against God Makes war with the saints Rev. 13:6, 7	Tribulation Saints killed Nation against nation Kingdom against kingdom Time of trouble such as never was Matt. 24:7-10, 21
Kingdom of Christ and The Saints	Stone Cut Out Without Hand Becomes Mountain Dan. 2:34, 35, 44, 45	JUDGMENT OF BEAST Saints possess the Kingdom Dan. 7:26, 27	ANTICHRIST DESTROYED Without Hand Dan. 8:25	Armies gathered against Jerusalem ANTICHRIST COMES TO HIS END Dan. 11:44, 45	Antichrist cast into the lake of fire Rev. 19:20	Armies against Jerusalem Luke 21:20 Ezek. 38:8, 9; Zech. 14:2 Coming of Christ with the Saints Matt. 24:29-31

CHAPTER EIGHT
Daniel's Further Visions

This chapter is the first time Daniel returns to writing in the Hebrew language since chapter two, verse four. The entire section from 2:4 through 7:28 was written in Aramaic. I believe that the return to the Hebrew language shows God's intention to show Daniel what would happen primarily to the *Jewish* people in the latter days. Let's look closely at the important details given to Daniel.

We saw in chapter seven that Daniel's vision covered a lengthy stretch of history from the Babylonian Empire unto the return of Christ. Now we are ready to take a more detailed look at that great vision and fill in some fascinating events. The purpose of a new vision is always to add details that have not been given in the past; each vision covers a little more ground than the previous one.

Let's look first at *when* this vision was given to Daniel:

> *In the third year of the reign of king*
> *Belshazzar a vision appeared unto me,*
> *even unto me Daniel, after that which*
> *appeared unto me at the first* (Daniel 8:1).

The vision given to Daniel in this chapter was in the year of the fall of Babylon, two years after his vision in chapter seven (see Daniel 7:1).

For the events of this vision, Daniel was transported in spirit to Shushan, the capital of Persia:

> *And I saw in a vision; and it came to*
> *pass, when I saw, that I was at Shushan*
> *in the palace, which is in the province of*
> *Elam; and I saw in a vision, and I was*
> *by the river of Ulai* (Daniel 8:2).

In this new vision of chapter eight, the bear of chapter

NOTES

seven becomes a ram; the leopard of chapter seven becomes a he goat in chapter eight. The HARMONY OF DANIEL'S EMPIRE VISIONS chart on page 82 will help you see the overall picture of these visions. Although we have a changing of images in this vision, we are not left to guessing in interpreting their proper meanings, because Daniel was given the divine interpretation through the agency of two "saints," a word more accurately translated "holy ones"—meaning angels.

In verse 16 Daniel is privileged to hear the name of an angel—Gabriel—revealed for the first time in the Bible. Daniel's spiritual PERCEPTION enabled him to hear things from God that no man before him had heard! The angel Gabriel reveals the divine interpretation of this vision to Daniel:

> *And it came to pass, when I, even I Daniel, had seen the vision, and sought for the meaning, then, behold, there stood before me as the appearance of a man. And I heard a man's voice between the banks of Ulai, which called, and said, Gabriel, make this man to understand the vision. So he came near where I stood: and when he came, I was afraid, and fell upon my face: but he said unto me, Understand, O son of man: for at the time of the end shall be the vision. Now as he was speaking with me, I was in a deep sleep on my face toward the ground: but he touched me, and set me upright. And he said, Behold, I will make thee know what shall be in the last end of the indignation: for at the time appointed the end shall be* (Daniel 8:15-19).

This is not the only instance of angels interpreting God's message; Zechariah had an angel talk with him to explain the many visions he received from the Lord:

> *Then said I, O my lord, what are these? And the angel that talked with me said unto me, I will shew thee what these be* (Zechariah 1:9).

And I said unto the angel that talked with me, What be these? And he answered me, These are the horns which have scattered Judah, Israel, and Jerusalem (Zechariah 1:19).

And, behold, the angel that talked with me went forth, and another angel went out to meet him, And said unto him, Run, speak to this young man, saying, Jerusalem shall be inhabited as towns without walls for the multitude of men and cattle therein (Zechariah 2:3,4).

God wants us to understand Daniel's visions, therefore He gives the interpretation through His angel:

VISION   *INTERPRETATION*

Then I lifted up mine eyes, and saw, and, behold, there stood before the river a ram which had two horns: and the two horns were high; but one was higher than the other, and the higher came up last. I saw the ram pushing westward, and northward, and southward; so that no beasts might stand before him, neither was there any that could deliver out of his hand; but he did according to his will, and became great (Daniel 8:3,4).

The ram which thou sawest having two horns are the kings of Media and Persia (Daniel 8:20).

NOTES

NOTES

VISION

And as I was considering, behold, an he goat came from the west on the face of the whole earth, and touched not the ground: and the goat had a notable horn between his eyes. And he came to the ram that had two horns, which I had seen standing before the river, and ran unto him in the fury of his power. And I saw him come close unto the ram, and he was moved with choler against him, and smote the ram, and brake his two horns: and there was no power in the ram to stand before him, but he cast him down to the ground, and stamped upon him: and there was none that could deliver the ram out of his hand (Daniel 8:5-7).

Therefore the he goat waxed very great: and when he was strong, the great horn was broken; and for it came

INTERPRETATION

And the rough goat is the king of Grecia: and the great horn that is between his eyes is the first king (Daniel 8:21).

Now that being broken, whereas four stood up for it, four kingdoms shall stand up out of the nation, but not

VISION	INTERPRETATION	NOTES

VISION

up four notable ones toward the four winds of heaven (Daniel 8:8).

And out of one of them came forth a little horn, which waxed exceeding great, toward the south, and toward the east, and toward the pleasant land (Daniel 8:9).

And it waxed great, even to the host of heaven; and it cast down some of the host and of the stars to the ground, and stamped upon them. Yea, he magnified himself even to the prince of the host, and by him the daily sacrifice was taken away, and the place of his sanctuary was cast down. And an host was given him against the daily sacrifice by reason of transgression, and it cast down the truth to the ground; and it practised, and prospered (Daniel 8:10-12).

INTERPRETATION

in his power (Daniel 8:22).

And in the latter time of their kingdom, when the transgressors are come to the full, a king of fierce countenance, and understanding dark sentences, shall stand up (Daniel 8:23).

And his power shall be mighty, but not by his own power: and he shall destroy wonderfully, and shall prosper, and practise, and shall destroy the mighty and the holy people. And through his policy also he shall cause craft to prosper in his hand; and he shall magnify himself in his heart, and by peace shall destroy many: he shall also stand up against the Prince of princes; but he shall be broken without hand (Daniel 8:24,25).

Then I heard one saint speaking, and another saint said unto that certain saint which spake, How long shall be the vision concerning the daily sacrifice, and the transgression of desolation, to give both the sanctuary and the host to be trodden under foot? And he said unto me, Unto two thousand and three hundred days; then shall the sanctuary be cleansed (Daniel 8:13,14).

NOTES

Daniel's reaction to this great vision was temporary weakness due to the anointing of the Lord:

And the vision of the evening and the morning which was told is true: wherefore shut thou up the vision; for it shall be for many days. And I Daniel fainted, and was sick certain days; afterward I rose up, and did the king's business; and I was astonished at the vision, but none understood it (Daniel 8:26,27).

History certainly verified Daniel's vision and the interpretation. The ram of verse 3 had two horns, representing the combined empires of the Medes and the Persians. The second horn was higher than the first horn, which clearly is a picture of the stronger Persian Empire having dominance over the Medes who preceded them.

We are told in verse 21 that the he goat represents the king or kingdom of Greece, and the "notable horn" of this he goat is its first king—Alexander the Great. The goat has been the symbol of Greece since its inception; its ancient capital was called *Aegea,* meaning "the goat city." The details concerning this kingdom closely match the historical record of Alexander's conquests.

The goat comes from the west (Greece) in its conquests (verse 5). He "touched not the ground," indicating the rapidity of Alexander's conquests; beginning at the age of only 20, he conquered a vast area before his death at 33 years old.

Verse 8 speaks of Alexander's death: " . . . *the great horn was broken; . . . .*" After his death, the empire was eventually divided between four of his generals. We have already seen this division which is also mentioned in verse 8: " . . . *for it came up four notable ones toward the four winds of heaven.*"

By comparing verse 9 and verse 23, we can see that the Antichrist is in view. It is "out of" one of these four areas of the Greek Empire that the Antichrist will arise in the last days. His desire is "toward the pleasant land" or Jerusalem (verse 9). Palestine or Israel has always been a prize for the major empires of the world to occupy. Isaiah spoke of Israel's prominence in the last days:

And it shall come to pass in the last days, that the mountain of the LORD'S house shall be established in the top of the mountains, and shall be exalted above the hills; and all nations shall flow unto it. And many people shall go and say, Come ye, and let us go up to the mountain of the LORD, to the house of the God of Jacob; and he will teach us of his ways, and we will walk in his paths: for out of Zion shall go forth the law, and the word of the LORD from Jerusalem (Isaiah 2:2,3).

Daniel 8:10-12 and verses 24 and 25 give us details of the Antichrist's reign:

The Antichrist starts with persecution of the godly (verse 10).

The Antichrist makes a covenant (KJV "policy") with the Jews (verse 25).

The Antichrist promises peace for the world and causes people to know how to prosper materially—he gains their dependence (verse 25).

The Antichrist will rebuild the city of Babylon (Revelation 18).

The Antichrist sets up ecclesiastical Babylon (Revelation 17).

The Antichrist calls himself the Messiah, breaks the covenant, and causes the daily sacrifice in the Temple to cease (verse 11).

The Antichrist sets up an idol of himself—the "abomination of desolation"—and casts down the Temple (verses 11-13).

The Antichrist is eventually destroyed "without hand" when he comes against Jesus Christ—the "Prince of

NOTES

89

NOTES

princes" (verse 25). (See also Revelation 17:14 and 19:11-21.)

Let's remember that God is revealing all these things to us so that we can be prepared. Satan is hard at work to thwart God's eternal purpose, but " . . . *we are not ignorant of* [Satan's] *devices*" (II Corinthians 2:11).

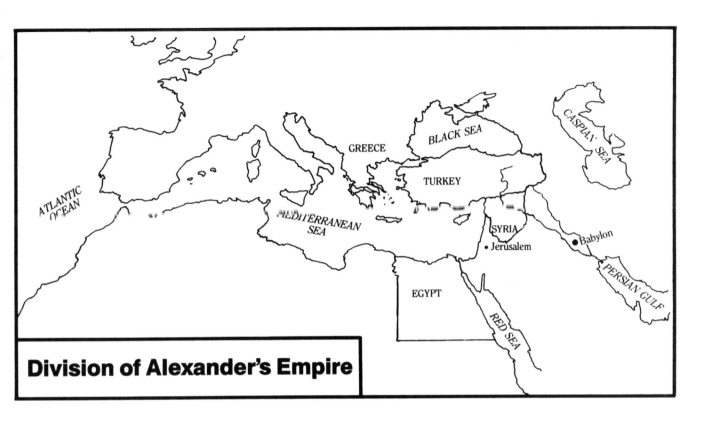

Division of Alexander's Empire

CHAPTER NINE
Daniel and the 70 Weeks

Daniel had in his possession portions of God's Word as it had been written by Jeremiah. Daniel was aware of Jeremiah's prophecy concerning the return of the Jewish captives at the end of 70 years' dispersion. Jeremiah had proclaimed this very plainly:

And this whole land shall be a desolation, and an astonishment; and these nations shall serve the king of Babylon seventy years (Jeremiah 25:11).

Thus saith the LORD of hosts, the God of Israel, unto all that are carried away captives, whom I have caused to be carried away from Jerusalem unto Babylon; Build ye houses, and dwell in them; and plant gardens, and eat the fruit of them; Take ye wives, and beget sons and daughters; and take wives for your sons, and give your daughters to husbands, that they may bear sons and daughters; that ye may be increased there, and not diminished. And seek the peace of the city whither I have caused you to be carried away captives, and pray unto the LORD for it: for in the peace thereof shall ye have peace.

For thus saith the LORD of hosts, the God of Israel; Let not your prophets and your diviners, that be in the midst of you, deceive you, neither hearken to your dreams which ye cause to be dreamed. For they prophesy falsely unto you in my name: I have not sent them, saith the LORD. For thus saith the LORD, that after seventy years be accomplished at Babylon I will visit you, and perform my good

NOTES

*word toward you, in causing you to
return to this place* (Jeremiah 29:4-10).

Daniel probably was taken into captivity in B.C. 606. By the time of this narrative in chapter 9, it would have been close to 68 years that had passed. Daniel also knew that Cyrus would sign a decree to let God's people return to the Promised Land:

*That saith of Cyrus, He is my shepherd,
and shall perform all my pleasure: even
saying to Jerusalem, Thou shalt be built;
and to the temple, Thy foundation shall
be laid* (Isaiah 44:28).

*Thus saith the LORD to his anointed, to
Cyrus, whose right hand I have holden,
to subdue nations before him; and I will
loose the loins of kings, to open before
him the two leaved gates; and the gates
shall not be shut* (Isaiah 45:1).

Daniel knew that the way to see God's promises come to pass in his people's lives was through prayer—to literally *pray the promises.* Therefore, he gave himself to prayer. God had promised very clearly that if His people repented and turned to Him, He would forgive them and restore them to their land:

*If they shall confess their iniquity, and the
iniquity of their fathers, with their
trespass which they trespassed against
me, and that also they have walked contrary*

unto me; And that I also have walked contrary unto them, and have brought them into the land of their enemies; if then their uncircumcised hearts be humbled, and they then accept of the punishment of their iniquity: Then will I remember my covenant with Jacob, and also my covenant with Isaac, and also my covenant with Abraham will I remember; and I will remember the land.

The land also shall be left of them, and shall enjoy her sabbaths, while she lieth desolate without them: and they shall accept of the punishment of their iniquity: because, even because they despised my judgments, and because their soul abhorred my statutes. And yet for all that, when they be in the land of their enemies, I will not cast them away, neither will I abhor them, to destroy them utterly, and to break my covenant with them: for I am the LORD their God. But I will for their sakes remember the covenant of their ancestors, whom I brought forth out of the land of Egypt in the sight of the heathen, that I might be their God: I am the LORD (Leviticus 26:40-45).

And it shall come to pass, when all these things are come upon thee, the blessing and the curse, which I have set before thee, and thou shalt call them to mind among all the nations, whither the LORD thy God hath driven thee, And shalt return unto the LORD thy God, and shalt obey his voice according to all that I command thee this day, thou and thy children, with all thine heart, and with all thy soul; That then the LORD thy God will turn thy captivity, and have compassion upon thee, and will return and gather thee from all the nations, whither the

NOTES

LORD thy God hath scattered thee. If any of thine be driven out unto the outmost parts of heaven, from thence will the LORD thy God gather thee, and from thence will he fetch thee: And the LORD thy God will bring thee into the land which thy fathers possessed, and thou shalt possess it; and he will do thee good, and multiply thee above thy fathers. And the LORD thy God will circumcise thine heart, and the heart of thy seed, to love the LORD thy God with all thine heart, and with all thy soul, that thou mayest live.

And the LORD thy God will put all these curses upon thine enemies, and on them that hate thee, which persecuted thee. And thou shalt return and obey the voice of the LORD, and do all his commandments which I command thee this day. And the LORD thy God will make thee plenteous in every work of thine hand, in the fruit of thy body, and in the fruit of thy cattle, and in the fruit of thy land, for good: for the LORD will again rejoice over thee for good, as he rejoiced over thy fathers: If thou shalt hearken unto the voice of the LORD thy God to keep his commandments and his statutes which are written in this book of the law, and if thou turn unto the LORD thy God with all thine heart, and with all thy soul (Deuteronomy 30:1-10).

In Daniel's extended prayer (Daniel 9:3-19) we see that he intercedes for his nation by confessing their sinful pattern (of course identifying himself with them) and cries out for God to intervene. An identity with the people and their sinfulness reminds us also of Moses and his identity with the people in Exodus 32 and 33. We are also reminded of how the apostle Paul prayed that he would be accursed so that his people might be saved:

For I could wish that myself were accursed from Christ for my brethren, my kinsmen according to the flesh (Romans 9:3).

At the time of the evening oblation, Daniel's prayers were interrupted:

Yea, whiles I was speaking in prayer, even the man Gabriel, whom I had seen in the vision at the beginning, being caused to fly swiftly, touched me about the time of the evening oblation (Daniel 9:21).

The evening oblation would be about 3:00 p.m. Of course, there was no Jewish temple in Babylon, and the one in Jerusalem had been destroyed. However, this was Daniel's usual time of prayer because it had been the time of prayer from his youth. That which Daniel learned as a boy remained with him a lifetime!

Gabriel came with a message telling Daniel that he was greatly beloved in heaven:

At the beginning of thy supplications the commandment came forth, and I am come to shew thee; for thou art greatly beloved: therefore understand the matter, and consider the vision (Daniel 9:23).

Gabriel came to tell Daniel of more than just the 70 weeks; he also came to show him God's plan and purpose for world affairs, as we shall see in chapters 10-12.

Let's look closely at the words of the angel:

Seventy weeks are determined upon thy people and upon thy holy city, to finish the transgression, and to make an end of sins, and to make reconciliation for iniquity, and to bring in everlasting righteousness, and to seal up the vision and prophecy, and to anoint the most Holy (Daniel 9:24).

To begin with, the angel tells Daniel the purpose of the 70 weeks. The key that will unlock the 70 weeks to us is that they cover the period when the Jews are dwelling in their own land.

There are six purposes for the 70 weeks:

(1) " . . . *to finish the transgression*, ..." This refers to the transgression of the Jews in Jerusalem and their disfavor with God. This will not be finished until they as a nation repent and turn to God.

(2) " . . . *to make an end of sins*, ..." This refers to restraining it, to stopping ungodliness from Jacob, to taking Israel away from their sins. This can only happen when their Deliverer comes—Jesus at his Second Coming:

And so all Israel shall be saved: as it is written, There shall come out of Sion the

*deliverer, and shall turn away ungodliness
from Jacob: For this is my covenant unto
them, when I shall take away their sins*
(Romans 11:26,27).

(3) " . . . *to make reconciliation for iniquity . . . .*"
The Jews will see that only One took their iniquity, and
they will see it at His Second Coming:

*Behold, he cometh with clouds; and every
eye shall see him, and they also which
pierced him: and all kindreds of the earth
shall wail because of him. Even so, Amen*
(Revelation 1:7).

*Who hath heard such a thing? Who hath
seen such things? Shall the earth be
made to bring forth in one day? or shall
a nation be born at once? for as soon as
Zion travailed, she brought forth her
children* (Isaiah 66:8).

*In that day there shall be a fountain
opened to the house of David and to the
inhabitants of Jerusalem for sin and for
uncleanness* (Zechariah 13:1).

*All we like sheep have gone astray; we
have turned every one to his own way;
and the LORD hath laid on him the iniquity
of us all* (Isaiah 53:6).

*For ye are all the children of God by
faith in Christ Jesus. For as many of you
as have been baptized into Christ have
put on Christ. There is neither Jew nor
Greek, there is neither bond nor free, there
is neither male nor female: for ye are all
one in Christ Jesus* (Galatians 3:26-28).

*And have put on the new man, which is
renewed in knowledge after the image of
him that created him: Where there is
neither Greek nor Jew, circumcision nor*

99

NOTES

uncircumcision, Barbarian, Scythian, bond nor free: but Christ is all, and in all (Colossians 3:10,11).

(4) ". . . to bring in everlasting righteousness, ..." Only with the new covenant can Israel be saved:

> But this shall be the covenant that I will make with the house of Israel; After those days, saith the LORD, I will put my law in their inward parts, and write it in their hearts; and will be their God, and they shall be my people. And they shall teach no more every man his neighbour, and every man his brother, saying, Know the LORD: for they shall all know me, from the least of them unto the greatest of them, saith the LORD: for I will forgive their iniquity, and I will remember their sin no more (Jeremiah 31:33,34).

(5) ". . . to seal up the vision and prophecy, ..." Vision and prophecy have to do with the Jewish people. When these visions and prophecies have been completed, they will be sealed up for preservation:

> For I would not, brethren, that ye should be ignorant of this mystery, lest ye should be wise in your own conceits; that blindness in part is happened to Israel, until the fulness of the Gentiles be come in (Romans 11:25).

> Charity never faileth: but whether there be prophecies, they shall fail; whether there be tongues, they shall cease; whether there be knowledge, it shall vanish away. For we know in part, and we prophesy in part. But when that which is perfect is come, then that which is in part shall be done away (I Corinthians 13:8-10).

(6) ". . . to anoint the most Holy." The "most Holy" is a place and not a person. Undoubtedly this refers to the

Millennial Temple. This is described in Ezekiel 41 and 42. The glory of God shall come back as the Jews knew it at one time in their past:

Then a cloud covered the tent of the congregation, and the glory of the LORD filled the tabernacle. And Moses was not able to enter into the tent of the congregation, because the cloud abode thereon, and the glory of the LORD filled the tabernacle (Exodus 40:34,35).

And they shall make an ark of shittim wood: two cubits and a half shall be the length thereof, and a cubit and a half the breadth thereof, and a cubit and a half the height thereof. And thou shalt overlay it with pure gold, within and without shalt thou overlay it, and shalt make upon it a crown of gold round about. And thou shalt cast four rings of gold for it, and put them in the four corners thereof; and two rings shall be in the one side of it, and two rings in the other side of it. And thou shalt make staves of shittim wood, and overlay them with gold. And thou shalt put the staves into the rings by the sides of the ark, that the ark may be borne with them. The staves shall be in the rings of the ark: they shall not be taken from it. And thou shalt put into the ark the testimony which I shall give thee.

And thou shalt make a mercy seat of pure gold: two cubits and a half shall be the length thereof, and a cubit and a half the breadth thereof. And thou shalt make two cherubims of gold, of beaten work shalt thou make them, in the two ends of the mercy seat. And make one cherub on the one end, and the other cherub on the other end: even of the mercy seat shall ye make the cherubims on the two ends thereof. And the cherubims shall stretch

101

NOTES

forth their wings on high, covering the mercy seat with their wings, and their faces shall look one to another; toward the mercy seat shall the faces of the cherubims be. And thou shalt put the mercy seat above upon the ark; and in the ark thou shalt put the testimony that I shall give thee. And there I will meet with thee, and I will commune with thee from above the mercy seat, from between the two cherubims which are upon the ark of the testimony, of all things which I will give thee in commandment unto the children of Israel (Exodus 25:10-22).

And when Moses was gone into the tabernacle of the congregation to speak with him, then he heard the voice of one speaking unto him from off the mercy seat that was upon the ark of testimony, from between the two cherubims: and he spake unto him (Numbers 7:89).

And it came to pass, when the priests were come out of the holy place, that the cloud filled the house of the LORD, So that the priests could not stand to minister because of the cloud: for the glory of the LORD had filled the house of the LORD (I Kings 8:10-11).

And the glory of the God of Israel was gone up from the cherub, whereupon he was, to the threshold of the house. And he called to the man clothed with linen, which had the writer's inkhorn by his side (Ezekiel 9:3).

And the glory of the LORD went up from the midst of the city, and stood upon the mountain which is on the east side of the city (Ezekiel 11:23).

Afterward he brought me to the gate, even the gate that looketh toward the east: And, behold, the glory of the God of Israel came from the way of the east: and his voice was like a noise of many waters: and the earth shined with his glory. And it was according to the appearance of the vision which I saw, even according to the vision that I saw when I came to destroy the city: and the visions were like the vision that I saw by the river Chebar; and I fell upon my face. And the glory of the LORD came into the house by the way of the gate whose prospect is toward the east. So the spirit took me up, and brought me into the inner court; and, behold, the glory of the LORD filled the house. And I heard him speaking unto me out of the house; and the man stood by me (Ezekiel 43:1-6).

We see very clearly that the six-fold purpose of the 70 weeks has to do with Israel. In looking at the 70 weeks, we see that the number 7 is a perfect number: it is composed of the divine number 3, which is the Father, Son, and the Holy Spirit, and the world number 4, which always has to do with earthly things like the four corners of the world and the four seasons.

NOTES

These "seventy weeks" are actually seventy weeks of days with each day representing one year:

> *After the number of the days in which ye searched the land, even forty days, each day for a year, shall ye bear your iniquities, even forty years, and ye shall know my breach of promise* (Numbers 14:34).

The seventy weeks are divided into segments:

> *Know therefore and understand, that from the going forth of the commandment to restore and to build Jerusalem unto the Messiah the Prince shall be seven weeks, and threescore and two weeks: the street shall be built again, and the wall, even in troublous times* (Daniel 9:25).

The first segment was seven weeks or 49 years. It took the Israelites 49 years to see the street and wall built when they returned to Jerusalem.

The first decree issued to allow the Jews to rebuild their Temple was signed by Cyrus:

> *Now in the first year of Cyrus king of Persia, that the word of the LORD by the mouth of Jeremiah might be fulfilled, the LORD stirred up the spirit of Cyrus king of Persia, that he made a proclamation throughout all his kingdom, and put it also in writing, saying, Thus saith Cyrus king of Persia, The LORD God of heaven hath given me all the kingdoms of the earth; and he hath charged me to build him an house at Jerusalem, which is in Judah. Who is there among you of all his people? his God be with him, and let him go up to Jerusalem, which is in Judah, and build the house of the LORD God of Israel, (he is the God,) which is in Jerusalem. And whosoever remaineth in any place where he sojourneth, let the men*

of his place help him with silver, and with
gold, and with goods, and with beasts,
beside the freewill offering for the house
of God that is in Jerusalem (Ezra 1:1-4).

At that time Cyrus issued a decree, and 50,000 captives returned to Jerusalem:

The whole congregation together was forty
and two thousand three hundred and
threescore, Beside their servants and their
maids, of whom there were seven thousand
three hundred thirty and seven: and there
were among them two hundred singing
men and singing women (Ezra 2:64,65).

A second decree was issued by Darius and is recorded in Ezra 5:1-17 and Ezra 6:1-12. Following the first decree the Israelites went back and built the Temple, but they were not involved in restoring and rebuilding Jerusalem. They do not finish building the Temple because their work was interfered with by the local people.

Their enemies sent to the king and told him to stop the Jews from rebuilding the Temple. At that time the Jews stopped building until Haggai and Zechariah rose up and prophesied to the people and built them up, cheered them up, and stirred them up to continue the building.

Darius then sent a decree after he found the decree of Cyrus and told the returned exiles to continue their building. The king even helped financially with the building of the Temple, and he told the Jews to restore and rebuild their city.

Artaxerxes, king of Persia, also helped the Jews who returned (Ezra 7:11-22). Then, as recorded in Nehemiah 2:1-8, Nehemiah, the cup bearer of the Persian court, was given permission to return to Jerusalem and help build the wall. It took Nehemiah and the people only 52 days to finish the wall. Nehemiah returned to Persia, but he had to make a second trip to Jerusalem to reestablish the law many years later.

The second segment of the prophecy concerning the

NOTES

NOTES

70 weeks is " . . . *seven weeks, and threescore and two weeks: . . . .*" This is 7 plus 62, which equals 69 weeks, and on the year/day scale totals 483 years. It was a total of 483 years from the issuance of the decree to Nehemiah until Jesus was crucified.

Undoubtedly there is a lapse of time between the 69th and 70th week. The first seven weeks or 49 years is the time it took the returned exiles to rebuild the Temple and reestablish their worship. The next 62 weeks come up to the time of Christ.

We are in no way dealing with the Church—only with the Jews.

After the 69th week the Jews were scattered abroad. Daniel 9:26 looks ahead to the Antichrist who will break his covenant with the Jews and commit the "abomination of desolation":

> *And after threescore and two weeks shall Messiah be cut off, but not for himself: and the people of the prince* [Antichrist] *that shall come shall destroy the city and the sanctuary; and the end thereof shall be with a flood, and unto the end of the war desolations are determined* (Daniel 9:26).

During the first half of Daniel's 70th week (3 and 1/2 years), the "prince" that shall come (the Antichrist) will make a 7-year covenant with the Jews. In the middle of the seven years he will break the covenant and cause the sacrifice and oblations to cease:

> *And he shall confirm the covenant with many for one week: and in the midst of the week he shall cause the sacrifice and the oblation to cease, and for the over-spreading of abominations he shall make it desolate, even until the consummation, and that determined shall be poured upon the desolate* (Daniel 9:27).

The last 3 and 1/2 years of the Tribulation will be the period of desolation. It is easily compared to Matthew 24:1-31.

106

The first half includes wars, famines, pestilences, earth-quakes, and false christs (Matthew 24:4-14).

In the middle of these verses in Matthew 24, we see the appearance of the abomination of desolation spoken of by Daniel:

> *When ye therefore shall see the abomination of desolation, spoken of by Daniel the prophet, stand in the holy place, (whoso readeth, let him understand:) Then let them which be in Judaea flee into the mountains: Let him which is on the housetop not come down to take any thing out of his house: Neither let him which is in the field return back to take his clothes. And woe unto them that are with child, and to them that give suck in those days! (Matthew 24:15-19).*

In the last half of Matthew 24 we see the period of tribulation such as there has never been before:

> *But pray ye that your flight be not in the winter, neither on the sabbath day: For then shall be great tribulation, such as was not since the beginning of the world to this time, no, nor ever shall be (Matthew 24:20,21).*

And then, of course, we see the arrival of Jesus in His Second Advent:

> *Immediately after the tribulation of those days shall the sun be darkened, and the moon shall not give her light, and the stars shall fall from heaven, and the powers of the heavens shall be shaken: And then shall appear the sign of the Son of man in heaven: and then shall all the tribes of the earth mourn, and they shall see the Son of man coming in the clouds of heaven with power and great glory (Matthew 24:29,30).*

NOTES

107

Let's look at four things that happen in the gap between the 69th and 70th week:

> *And after threescore and two weeks shall Messiah be cut off, but not for himself: and the people of the prince* [Antichrist] *that shall come shall destroy the city and the sanctuary; and the end thereof shall be with a flood, and unto the end of the war desolations are determined* (Daniel 9:26).

(1) The Messiah is to be cut off (of course this is the Crucifixion), but not for Himself. We know that Jesus did not die for Himself, He died for others:

> *Who his own self bare our sins in his own body on the tree, that we, being dead to sins, should live unto righteousness: by whose stripes ye were healed* (I Peter 2:24).

(2) Jerusalem and the Temple will be destroyed.

(3) The prince that will come undoubtedly will be the Antichrist who will destroy the city and the sanctuary.

(4) Palestine shall be desolate until the Second Coming of Christ Who shall destroy the Antichrist.

We are certainly approaching the end of the Church age and the beginning of Israel's 70th week!

Daniel's 70 Weeks Chart

Decree of Cyrus (Ezra 1:1-4)	69 weeks (483 years)		Jesus crucified / Jews scattered	Church Age Gentiles / Rapture	1 week (7 yrs.) Tribulation
	7 weeks (49 yrs.) street and wall rebuilt	62 weeks			
	Daniel 9:25				Daniel 9:26

108

CHAPTER TEN
A Praying Saint

In Daniel chapter 10 we see a praying Daniel—praying and interceding concerning the return of his people to their Promised Land. Jeremiah had prophesied that they would return at the end of 70 years:

> *And this whole land shall be a desolation, and an astonishment; and these nations shall serve the king of Babylon seventy years* (Jeremiah 25:11).

In the first year of Cyrus, the king of Persia, the Lord stirred up Cyrus to make a proclamation that the Jews should return to build their Temple at Jerusalem:

> *Now in the first year of Cyrus king of Persia, that the word of the LORD by the mouth of Jeremiah might be fulfilled, the LORD stirred up the spirit of Cyrus king of Persia, that he made a proclamation throughout all his kingdom, and put it also in writing, saying, Thus saith Cyrus king of Persia, The LORD God of heaven hath given me all the kingdoms of the earth; and he hath charged me to build him an house at Jerusalem, which is in Judah* (Ezra 1:1,2).

It was prophesied by Isaiah, almost 150 years before the birth of Cyrus, that this Persian king would do this very thing:

> *That saith of Cyrus, He is my shepherd, and shall perform all my pleasure: even saying to Jerusalem, Thou shalt be built; and to the temple, Thy foundation shall be laid* (Isaiah 44:28).

NOTES

Thus saith the LORD to his anointed, to Cyrus, whose right hand I have holden, to subdue nations before him; and I will loose the loins of kings, to open before him the two leaved gates; and the gates shall not be shut; I will go before thee, and make the crooked places straight: I will break in pieces the gates of brass, and cut in sunder the bars of iron: And I will give thee the treasures of darkness, and hidden riches of secret places, that thou mayest know that I, the LORD, which call thee by thy name, am the God of Israel. For Jacob my servant's sake, and Israel mine elect, I have even called thee by thy name: I have surnamed thee, though thou hast not known me. I am the LORD, and there is none else, there is no God beside me: I girded thee, though thou hast not known me (Isaiah 45:1-5).

Those who chose to return to Israel took with them 5,400 vessels of gold and silver which had been taken by Nebuchadnezzar in the three captivities:

All the vessels of gold and of silver were five thousand and four hundred. All these did Shesh-bazzar bring up with them of the captivity that were brought up from Babylon unto Jerusalem (Ezra 1:11).

In the first expedition over 24,000 Israelites returned. Detail is given of their names and their family pedigrees in

Ezra chapter two. This was a small number compared to the number who had been resettled in Babylon.

Another group returned later, but even the combined numbers brought the total who returned to perhaps a little over 44,000. This undoubtedly burdened the heart of Daniel, and he went into 21 days of fasting and prayer:

> *In those days I Daniel was mourning three full weeks. I ate no pleasant bread, neither came flesh nor wine in my mouth, neither did I anoint myself at all, till three whole weeks were fulfilled* (Daniel 10:2,3).

This was probably not a total fast; perhaps he refrained from proteins and simply lived on fruit or fruit juices.

Beginning in verse five I believe that Daniel received a visitation from the Lord Jesus Christ:

> *Then I lifted up mine eyes, and looked, and behold a certain man clothed in linen, whose loins were girded with fine gold of Uphaz: His body also was like the beryl, and his face as the appearance of lightning, and his eyes as lamps of fire, and his arms and his feet like in colour to polished brass, and the voice of his words like the voice of a multitude* (Daniel 10:5,6).

> *And I turned to see the voice that spake with me. And being turned, I saw seven golden candlesticks; And in the midst of the seven candlesticks one like unto the*

111

Son of man, clothed with a garment down to the foot, and girt about the paps with a golden girdle. His head and his hairs were white like wool, as white as snow; and his eyes were as a flame of fire; And his feet like unto fine brass, as if they burned in a furnace; and his voice as the sound of many waters (Revelation 1:12-15).

I believe that this was an appearance of the preincarnate Jesus just as it was in Genesis 18:1-8 and Exodus 3:1-6,13,14.

When Daniel experienced his great vision, he lost all strength to stand and fell with his face on the ground. This is the same reaction that Paul had when the Lord appeared to him on the way to Damascus:

And as he journeyed, he came near Damascus: and suddenly there shined round about him a light from heaven: And he fell to the earth, and heard a voice saying unto him, Saul, Saul, why persecutest thou me? (Acts 9:3,4).

Next, a heavenly messenger, Gabriel, appeared to Daniel:

And, behold, an hand touched me, which set me upon my knees and upon the palms of my hands. And he said unto me,

*O Daniel, a man greatly beloved, understand
the words that I speak unto thee, and
stand upright: for unto thee am I now
sent. And when he had spoken this word
unto me, I stood trembling* (Daniel 10:10,11).

God often sends an interpreting angel to go with the visions
He gives to His saints. This is clearly seen in the book of
Zechariah. Gabriel was sent here for the purpose of being
an interpreting angel.

Beginning with Daniel 10:12 we have the curtain of
heaven pulled back, and we are given a very intimate view
of what happens between heaven and earth when men and
women pray. In this account we see the star wars that
literally go on in heaven. The star wars began with the fall
of Satan and will continue till the new heaven and the
new earth.

Our contact between heaven and earth is the wonderful
Holy Spirit:

*Howbeit when he, the Spirit of truth, is
come, he will guide you into all truth: for
he shall not speak of himself; but whatsoever he shall hear, that shall he speak:
and he will shew you things to come*
(John 16:13).

Satan is called the "prince of the power of the air":

NOTES

113

Wherein in time past ye walked according to the course of this world, according to the prince of the power of the air, the spirit that now worketh in the children of disobedience (Ephesians 2:2).

Jesus also called him the "prince of this world":

Hereafter I will not talk much with you: for the prince of this world cometh, and hath nothing in me (John 14:30).

There is no question that Satan has an organized government—principalities and powers, rulers of darkness, and spiritual wickedness in high places. I believe the prince of the kingdom of Persia is Satan's leader of wickedness in high places. Undoubtedly high ranking evil spirits are appointed over nations.

Gabriel had been detained 21 days—the length of the time of Daniel's prayer. Michael, another archangel, came to his rescue, or Gabriel would not have arrived when he did:

But the prince of the kingdom of Persia withstood me one and twenty days: but, lo, Michael, one of the chief princes, came to help me; and I remained there with the kings of Persia (Daniel 10:13).

Michael is also mentioned in Jude 9:

Yet Michael the archangel, when contending
with the devil he disputed about the body
of Moses, durst not bring against him a
railing accusation, but said, The Lord
rebuke thee (Jude 9).

So we see that there is a spirit world very much involved in the affairs of men and the nations which are upon this earth. There is a kingdom of darkness, and we cannot handle it in the flesh; it must be dealt with in the spirit:

For we wrestle not against flesh and
blood, but against principalities, against
powers, against the rulers of the darkness
of this world, against spiritual wickedness
in high places (Ephesians 6:12).

There was a very specific purpose to Gabriel's visit; he was to give Daniel understanding as to what would happen to his people. (I believe this means the Jewish people in the latter days.) Daniel not only lost his strength, but he also lost his tongue until his lips were touched:

And when he had spoken such words unto
me, I set my face toward the ground, and
I became dumb. And, behold, one like
the similitude of the sons of men touched
my lips: then I opened my mouth, and
spake, and said unto him that stood
before me, O my lord, by the vision my
sorrows are turned upon me, and I have
retained no strength (Daniel 10:15,16).

This is similar to the call of Isaiah:

Then flew one of the seraphims unto me,
having a live coal in his hand, which he
had taken with the tongs from off the
altar: And he laid it upon my mouth, and
said, Lo, this hath touched thy lips; and
thine iniquity is taken away, and thy sin
purged (Isaiah 6:6,7).

NOTES

Not only was his mouth touched, but his strength was once again given to him:

> *Then there came again and touched me one like the appearance of a man, and he strengthened me, And said, O man greatly beloved, fear not: peace be unto thee, be strong, yea, be strong. And when he had spoken unto me, I was strengthened, and said, Let my lord speak; for thou hast strengthened me* (Daniel 10:18,19).

The fact that Daniel is called "greatly beloved" is wonderful—to be known in heaven as "beloved" is to truly be known!

In verse 20 we see that Gabriel must return to heaven, and he will again fight with the prince of Persia because he is going through the powers of the air. This is why these powers have to be shaken; and they will be shaken—especially with the Rapture of the Church. Because of Michael and Gabriel the fall of Babylon was brought about in the time of Cyrus and Darius.

Daniel has four direct visions in this book: the vision of the four beasts in chapter 7; the vision of the ram and the he-goat in chapter 8; the vision of the seventy weeks in chapter 9; and the vision of Jesus and future events for Israel in chapters 10 through 12. The first vision shows the major gentile empires and the kingdom of Christ being established upon the earth; the last three visions give details of the Antichrist—his beginning, his works, his end, and his fall.

Before Gabriel leaves he gives last instructions to the beloved Daniel. Sometimes we feel that we are not beloved, but God writes our names in a book of remembrance when we fear and think upon His name:

> *Then they that feared the LORD spake often one to another: and the LORD hearkened, and heard it, and a book of remembrance was written before him for them that feared the LORD, and that thought upon his name* (Malachi 3:16).

Heaven is far from a primitive place. Complete records are kept; books will be opened in the latter time, and men will be judged by their works. Thank God, if you are a Christian, your name is written in the Lamb's book of life, the best book of all.

CHAPTER ELEVEN
Prophecy in Detail

No other portion of Scripture presents such detailed prophecy as this chapter. Verses 1-34 describe events from the time of Darius the Mede until Antiochus Epiphanes (around 150 B.C.). Verses 35-45 concern the end-time activities of the Antichrist.

PROPHECY	FULFILLMENT	NOTES

PROPHECY

Also I in the first year of Darius the Mede, even I, stood to confirm and to strengthen him (Daniel 11:1).

FULFILLMENT

The "I" of this verse is the angel Gabriel. Many consider this verse the last verse of chapter ten. At any rate, Daniel is told by Gabriel that the first year Darius the Mede took office, he (Gabriel) confirmed and strengthened the king on behalf of the Jews.

And now will I shew thee the truth. Behold, there shall stand up yet three kings in Persia; and the fourth shall be far richer than they all: and by his strength through his riches he shall stir up all against the realm of Grecia (Daniel 11:2).

The angel informs Daniel that there will be four more kings to rule over the Persian Empire before Alexander the Great comes on the scene. These four kings were (1) Cyrus, (2) Cambyses, the son of Cyrus, (3) Darius I, and (4) Xerxes. It is said by

119

NOTES

PROPHECY

FULFILLMENT

Greek authors that Xerxes had great wealth and an army of 800,000 men. He led his army against Greece, fulfilling verse two.

And a mighty king shall stand up, that shall rule with great dominion, and do according to his will (Daniel 11:3).

The "mighty king," of course, is Alexander the Great.

And when he shall stand up, his kingdom shall be broken, and shall be divided toward the four winds of heaven; and not to his posterity, nor according to his dominion which he ruled: for his kingdom shall be plucked up, even for others beside those (Daniel 11:4).

After reigning only 12 years, Alexander died during a drunken orgy. Within 15 years not one of his posterity was alive. Alexander's kingdom was eventually divided among four of his generals into what is now Turkey, Syria, Egypt, and Greece.

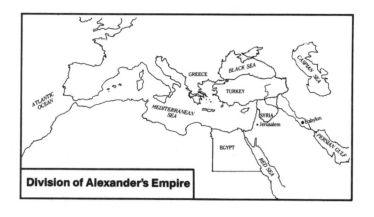

Division of Alexander's Empire

And the king of the south shall be strong, and one of his princes; and he shall be strong above him, and have dominion; his dominion shall be a great dominion (Daniel 11:5).

The "king of the south" would be Ptolemy I. He ruled Egypt upon the death of Alexander. The ruler of the northern kingdom ("*. . . he shall be strong above him, . . .*") was Seleucus I, the king of Syria.

PROPHECY	FULFILLMENT	NOTES

PROPHECY

And in the end of years they shall join themselves together; for the king's daughter of the south shall come to the king of the north to make an agreement: but she shall not retain the power of the arm; neither shall he stand, nor his arm: but she shall be given up, and they that brought her, and he that begat her, and he that strengthened her in these times (Daniel 11:6).

FULFILLMENT

After many years these two kingdoms made a league. The daughter (Berenice) of Ptolemy I (king of Egypt) married Antiochus Theos, king of Syria. She did not "retain the power" that her marriage brought, because Antiochus returned to his first wife (who later had him poisoned and Berenice murdered!).

But out of a branch of her roots shall one stand up in his estate, which shall come with an army, and shall enter into the fortress of the king of the north, and shall deal against them, and shall prevail: And shall also carry captives into Egypt their gods, with their princes, and with their precious vessels of silver and of gold; and he shall continue more years than the king of the north. So the king of the south shall come into his kingdom, and shall return into his own land (Daniel 11:7-9).

The "branch" spoken of here is the brother of Berenice, Ptolemy III, who avenged his sister's death by invading Syria and then returned to Egypt.

NOTES

PROPHECY

But his sons shall be stirred up, and shall assemble a multitude of great forces: and one shall certainly come, and overflow, and pass through: then shall he return, and be stirred up, even to his fortress. And the king of the south shall be moved with choler, and shall come forth and fight with him, even with the king of the north: and he shall set forth a great multitude; but the multitude shall be given into his hand. And when he hath taken away the multitude, his heart shall be lifted up; and he shall cast down many ten thousands: but he shall not be strengthened by it (Daniel 11:10-12).

For the king of the north shall return, and shall set forth a multitude greater than the former, and shall certainly come after certain years with a great army and with much riches. And in those times there shall many stand up against the king of the south: also the robbers of thy people shall exalt themselves to establish the vision; but they shall fall. So the king of the north shall come, and cast up a mount, and take the most fenced cities: and the arms of the south shall not withstand, neither his chosen people, neither shall there be any strength to withstand. But he that cometh against

FULFILLMENT

Later, the sons of Seleucus II, ruler of Syria, (Seleucus III and Antiochus the Great) attempted to go to war against Ptolemy III of Egypt. Ptolemy defeated Antiochus.

Antiochus the Great ("king of the north") returned after 14 years and this time defeated the current ruler of Egypt, Ptolemy V. Keep in mind that Israel is in the middle of these two kingdoms; in the warring between Syria and Egypt, Israel suffered.

122

NOTES

him shall do according to his own will, and none shall stand before him: and he shall stand in the glorious land, which by his hand shall be consumed (Daniel 11:13-16).

He shall also set his face to enter with the strength of his whole kingdom, and upright ones with him; thus shall he do: and he shall give him the daughter of women, corrupting her: but she shall not stand on his side, neither be for him (Daniel 11:17).

Antiochus the Great and Ptolemy V finally came into agreement. Antiochus gave Ptolemy his daughter; she later helped Ptolemy defeat her father.

After this shall he turn his face unto the isles, and shall take many: but a prince for his own behalf shall cause the reproach offered by him to cease; without his own reproach he shall cause it to turn upon him. Then he shall turn his face toward the fort of his own land: but he shall stumble and fall, and not be found (Daniel 11:18,19).

Antiochus turned his attention to Greece, was defeated there too, and returned to his homeland only to be slain in an attempt to plunder the temple of Jupiter Belus in his eastern province.

Then shall stand up in his estate a raiser of taxes in the glory of the kingdom: but within few days he shall be destroyed, neither in anger, nor in battle (Daniel 11:20).

The son of Antiochus the Great, Seleucus, succeeded his father and sought to rob the Temple at Jerusalem in his attempt to exact money from them to pay his annual tax to the Romans. He was poisoned by his treasurer, Heliodorus, who wanted to ascend to the throne.

And in his estate shall stand up a vile person, to whom

Seleucus was succeeded by Antiochus Epiphanes, who

PROPHECY

they shall not give the honour of the kingdom: but he shall come in peaceably, and obtain the kingdom by flatteries (Daniel 11:21).

And with the arms of a flood shall they be overflown from before him, and shall be broken; yea, also the prince of the covenant. And after the league made with him he shall work deceitfully: for he shall come up, and shall become strong with a small people. He shall enter peaceably even upon the fattest places of the province; and he shall do that which his fathers have not done, nor his fathers' fathers; he shall scatter among them the prey, and spoil, and riches: yea, and he shall forecast his devices against the strong holds, even for a time (Daniel 11:22-24).

And he shall stir up his power and his courage against the king of the south with a great army; and the king of the south shall be stirred up to battle with a very great and mighty army; but he shall not stand: for they shall forecast devices against him. Yea, they that feed of the portion of his meat shall destroy him, and his army shall overflow: and many shall fall down slain. And both these kings' hearts

FULFILLMENT

gained the throne through flattering authorities in Rome and nearby countries, thereby crushing Heliodorus. The true heir to the throne, Demetrius (another son of Seleucus IV), was a prisoner in Rome.

Antiochus overcame opposition in Israel and removed the high priest (Onias), replacing him with Jason (who had given Antiochus a large sum of money). Antiochus obtained the wealth of the people and became strong.

Antiochus made war with Ptolemy (ruler of Egypt) and defeated him. It was Ptolemy's own key men who helped bring about his downfall. Both of these rulers spoke lies and attempted to deceive one another.

PROPHECY	FULFILLMENT
shall be to do mischief, and they shall speak lies at one table; but it shall not prosper: for yet the end shall be at the time appointed (Daniel 11:25-27).	
Then shall he return into his land with great riches; and his heart shall be against the holy covenant; and he shall do exploits, and return to his own land (Daniel 11:28).	Antiochus returned to Syria. He heard that the citizens of Jerusalem rejoiced at a report (obviously false) of his death, and he therefore turned against his covenant with the Jews.
At the time appointed he shall return, and come toward the south; but it shall not be as the former, or as the latter. For the ships of Chittim shall come against him: therefore he shall be grieved, and return, and have indignation against the holy covenant: so shall he do; he shall even return, and have intelligence with them that forsake the holy covenant. And arms shall stand on his part, and they shall pollute the sanctuary of strength, and shall take away the daily sacrifice, and they shall place the abomination that maketh desolate (Daniel 11:29-31).	Antiochus began a second invasion of Egypt, only to be turned back by the Romans in conjunction with Cyprus (the "ships of Chittim"). In his anger, he turned against the Jews and, with the help of some apostate Jews, he plundered Jerusalem, killed a multitude of worshipers in the Temple, and later consecrated the Temple to Jupiter Olympius. He thus took away "the daily sacrifice." Apollonius, Antiochus' general, set up idols in the Temple and sacrificed swine within its walls—the "abomination that maketh desolate."

NOTES

NOTES

PROPHECY

And such as do wickedly against the covenant shall he corrupt by flatteries: but the people that do know their God shall be strong, and do exploits. And they that understand among the people shall instruct many: yet they shall fall by the sword, and by flame, by captivity, and by spoil, many days. Now when they shall fall, they shall be holpen with a little help: but many shall cleave to them with flatteries (Daniel 11:32-34).

And some of them of understanding shall fall, to try them, and to purge, and to make them white, even to the time of the end: because it is yet for a time appointed (Daniel 11:35).

And the king shall do according to his will; and he shall exalt himself, and magnify himself above every god, and shall speak marvellous things against the God of gods, and shall prosper till the indignation be accomplished: for that that is determined shall be done. Neither shall he regard the God of his fathers, nor the desire of women, nor regard any god: for he shall magnify himself above all. But in his estate shall he honour the God of forces: and a god whom his fathers knew not shall he honour with gold,

FULFILLMENT

Antiochus was resisted by the Maccabees and their followers. These brave people chose to suffer great persecution at the hand of Antiochus.

Verse 35 makes it clear that these visions have end-time applications.

A king equal to Antiochus Epiphanes will arise in the end times. This will be the Antichrist. He gives his life and power to Satan.

126

PROPHECY

and silver, and with precious stones, and pleasant things. Thus shall he do in the most strong holds with a strange god, whom he shall acknowledge and increase with glory: and he shall cause them to rule over many, and shall divide the land for gain (Daniel 11:36-39).

And at the time of the end shall the king of the south push at him: and the king of the north shall come against him like a whirlwind, with chariots, and with horsemen, and with many ships; and he shall enter into the countries, and shall overflow and pass over. He shall enter also into the glorious land, and many countries shall be overthrown: but these shall escape out of his hand, even Edom, and Moab, and the chief of the children of Ammon. He shall stretch forth his hand also upon the countries: and the land of Egypt shall not escape. But he shall have power over the treasures of gold and of silver, and over all the precious things of Egypt: and the Libyans and the Ethiopians shall be at his steps (Daniel 11:40-43).

But tidings out of the east and out of the north shall trouble him: therefore he shall go forth with great fury to

FULFILLMENT

The Antichrist will conquer Egypt, Greece, Turkey, and Syria. Edom, Moab, and Ammon will escape his rule; the Antichrist will not conquer the whole world. This will be the beginning of the Antichrist's reign over the ten kingdoms.

Nations of the east and of the north will come against the Antichrist, but he will conquer these and break his

NOTES

NOTES

PROPHECY

destroy, and utterly to make away many (Daniel 11:44).

And he shall plant the tabernacles of his palace between the seas in the glorious holy mountain; yet he shall come to his end, and none shall help him (Daniel 11:45).

FULFILLMENT

covenant with the Jews, resulting in "great fury to destroy."

The Antichrist attempts to establish his rule in the Temple at Jerusalem. His end will be the lake of fire (Revelation 19:20; 20:10).

This chapter is amazing proof of the inspiration of the Bible and of God's involvement in world affairs. The climax of Daniel's vision—the Great Tribulation and the Resurrection—is contained in chapter 12.

CHAPTER TWELVE

" . . . the end of the days."

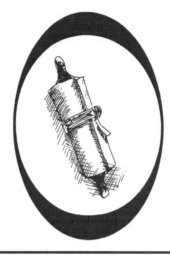

The last chapter of Daniel gives us details of the Tribulation period. We see that the archangel Michael stands up for the Jews during this time:

And at that time shall Michael stand up, the great prince which standeth for the children of thy people: and there shall be a time of trouble, such as never was since there was a nation even to that same time: and at that time thy people shall be delivered, every one that shall be found written in the book (Daniel 12:1).

In Jude 9 Michael is called an archangel:

Yet Michael the archangel, when contending with the devil he disputed about the body of Moses, durst not bring against him a railing accusation, but said, The Lord rebuke thee (Jude 9).

Michael is mentioned two other times in Daniel:

NOTES

129

But the prince of the kingdom of Persia withstood me one and twenty days: but, lo, Michael, one of the chief princes, came to help me; and I remained there with the kings of Persia (Daniel 10:13).

But I will shew thee that which is noted in the scripture of truth: and there is none that holdeth with me in these things, but Michael your prince (Daniel 10:21).

In the book of Revelation, Michael is in command of an angelic army in heaven:

And there was war in heaven: Michael and his angels fought against the dragon; and the dragon fought and his angels (Revelation 12:7).

Michael helps oust Satan's forces in the heavenlies and cast them down to the earth.

When the Antichrist appears following the Rapture (and I believe this is the timing of this account), he will harass the remnant of the Church who are left here during the first 3½ years of the Tribulation. But in the last 3½ years (which we are pinpointing in Daniel 12:1), he will harass the Jews. This will be the time of Jacob's trouble:

And these are the words that the LORD spake concerning Israel and concerning Judah. For thus saith the LORD; We have heard a voice of trembling, of fear, and not of peace. Ask ye now, and see whether a man doth travail with child? wherefore do I see every man with his hands on his loins, as a woman in travail, and all faces are turned into paleness? Alas! for that day is great, so that none is like it: it is even the time of Jacob's trouble; but he shall be saved out of it (Jeremiah 30:4-7).

Ezekiel says of this time that the Israelites "pass under the rod":

And I will bring you out from the people, and will gather you out of the countries wherein ye are scattered, with a mighty hand, and with a stretched out arm, and with fury poured out. And I will bring you into the wilderness of the people, and there will I plead with you face to face. Like as I pleaded with your fathers in the wilderness of the land of Egypt, so will I plead with you, saith the Lord GOD. And I will cause you to pass under the rod, and I will bring you into the bond of the covenant: And I will purge out from among you the rebels, and them that transgress against me: I will bring them forth out of the country where they sojourn, and they shall not enter into the land of Israel: and ye shall know that I am the LORD (Ezekiel 20:34-38).

Israel will be the melting pot:

Son of man, the house of Israel is to me become dross: all they are brass, and tin, and iron, and lead, in the midst of the furnace; they are even the dross of silver. Therefore thus saith the Lord GOD; Because ye are all become dross, behold, therefore I will gather you into the midst of Jerusalem. As they gather silver, and

NOTES

NOTES

brass, and iron, and lead, and tin, into the midst of the furnace, to blow the fire upon it, to melt it; so will I gather you in mine anger and in my fury, and I will leave you there, and melt you. Yea, I will gather you, and blow upon you in the fire of my wrath, and ye shall be melted in the midst thereof. As silver is melted in the midst of the furnace, so shall ye be melted in the midst thereof; and ye shall know that I the LORD have poured out my fury upon you (Ezekiel 22:18-22).

This is also mentioned by Zechariah:

And I will bring the third part through the fire, and will refine them as silver is refined, and will try them as gold is tried: they shall call on my name, and I will hear them: I will say, It is my people: and they shall say, The LORD is my God (Zechariah 13:9).

The last book of the Old Testament speaks of the first and second advent of Jesus and the purifying that He shall do to Israel:

Behold, I will send my messenger, and he shall prepare the way before me: and the Lord, whom ye seek, shall suddenly come to his temple, even the messenger of the covenant, whom ye delight in: behold, he shall come, saith the LORD of hosts. But who may abide the day of his coming? and who shall stand when he appeareth? for he is like a refiner's fire, and like fullers' soap: And he shall sit as a refiner and purifier of silver: and he shall purify the sons of Levi, and purge them as gold and silver, that they may offer unto the LORD an offering in righteousness (Malachi 3:1-3).

In Daniel 12:2 we read of the resurrection of the dead:

*And many of them that sleep in the dust
of the earth shall awake, some to
everlasting life, and some to shame and
everlasting contempt.*

According to Jude 9 Michael contested with the devil over the resurrection of Moses; it is probably Michael's voice that will be heard in connection with the resurrection mentioned by the apostle Paul:

*For the Lord himself shall descend from
heaven with a shout, with the voice of the
archangel, and with the trump of God:
and the dead in Christ shall rise first*
(I Thessalonians 4:16).

If Satan opposed the resurrection of Moses, he will certainly oppose the resurrection of the Body of Christ mentioned in Revelation 12:5:

*And she brought forth a man child, who
was to rule all nations with a rod of iron:
and her child was caught up unto God,
and to his throne* (Revelation 12:5).

Moses undoubtedly was raised from the dead because he, along with Elijah who was caught up, appeared on the Mount of Transfiguration in his glorified body:

*And was transfigured before them: and
his face did shine as the sun, and his raiment
was white as the light. And, behold, there
appeared unto them Moses and Elias
talking with him* (Matthew 17:2,3).

These will be the two witnesses in Revelation 11; they will represent the one who is caught up and the one raised from the dead. They will call down the very plagues in Revelation that they did in their time and in their earthly bodies as recorded in Exodus 5-12 and I Kings 17,18.

There are basically three kinds of resurrections in the Scripture:

NOTES

133

(1) There is a spiritual resurrection:

And you hath he quickened, who were dead in trespasses and sins; Even when we were dead in sins, hath quickened us together with Christ, (by grace ye are saved;) And hath raised us up together, and made us sit together in heavenly places in Christ Jesus (Ephesians 2:1,5,6).

Wherefore he saith, Awake thou that sleepest, and arise from the dead, and Christ shall give thee light (Ephesians 5:14).

Likewise reckon ye also yourselves to be dead indeed unto sin, but alive unto God through Jesus Christ our Lord (Romans 6:11).

Verily, verily, I say unto you, He that heareth my word, and believeth on him that sent me, hath everlasting life, and shall not come into condemnation; but is passed from death unto life (John 5:24).

(2) There is a physical resurrection:

Marvel not at this: for the hour is coming, in the which all that are in the graves shall hear his voice, And shall come forth; they that have done good, unto the resurrection of life; and they that have done evil, unto the resurrection of damnation (John 5:28-29).

(3) There is a national resurrection:

Therefore, behold, the days come, saith the LORD, that it shall no more be said, The LORD liveth, that brought up the children of Israel out of the land of Egypt; But, The LORD liveth, that brought up the children of Israel from the land of the north, and from all the lands whither he had driven them: and I will bring them again into their land that I gave unto their fathers (Jeremiah 16:14,15).

At this time the Jews will be restored to their own land, and all Israel shall be saved (Romans 11:26). There is no question there will be a national resurrection of the Jews—Ezekiel saw this in his vision of the dry bones:

Then he said unto me, Son of man, these bones are the whole house of Israel: behold, they say, Our bones are dried, and our hope is lost: we are cut off for our parts. Therefore prophesy and say unto them, Thus saith the Lord GOD; Behold, O my people, I will open your graves, and cause you to come up out of your graves, and bring you into the land of Israel. And say unto them, Thus saith the Lord GOD; Behold, I will take the children of Israel from among the heathen, whither they be gone, and will gather them on every side, and bring them into their own land: And I will make them one nation in the land upon the mountains of Israel; and one king shall be king to them all: and they shall be no more two nations, neither shall they be divided into two kingdoms any more at all (Ezekiel 37:11,12,21,22). (See also Ezekiel 48:1-29.)

During the last half of the Tribulation, the Jews will return to Christ:

And I will pour upon the house of David, and upon the inhabitants of Jerusalem, the spirit of grace and of supplications: and they shall look upon me whom they have pierced, and they shall mourn for him, as one mourneth for his only son, and shall be in bitterness for him, as one that is in bitterness for his firstborn (Zechariah 12:10).

NOTES

135

God will pour out a spirit of grace and supplication, and as a nation they will repent:

> *In that day shall there be a great mourning in Jerusalem, as the mourning of Hadad-rimmon in the valley of Megiddon. And the land shall mourn, every family apart; the family of the house of David apart, and their wives apart; the family of the house of Nathan apart, and their wives apart; The family of the house of Levi apart, and their wives apart; the family of Shimei apart, and their wives apart; All the families that remain, every family apart, and their wives apart* (Zechariah 12:11-14).

> *For I will take you from among the heathen, and gather you out of all countries, and will bring you into your own land. Then will I sprinkle clean water upon you, and ye shall be clean: from all your filthiness, and from all your idols, will I cleanse you. A new heart also will I give you, and a new spirit will I put within you: and I will take away the stony heart out of your flesh, and I will give you an heart of flesh. And I will put my spirit within you, and cause you to walk in my statutes, and ye shall keep my judgments, and do them* (Ezekiel 36:24-27).

> *Who hath heard such a thing? who hath seen such things? Shall the earth be made to bring forth in one day? or shall a nation be born at once? for as soon as Zion travailed, she brought forth her children* (Isaiah 66:8).

Truly a nation will be reborn in a day. God will take Judah and Israel again and make them one. Not all Jews will receive Christ; not all Jews will do a turnaround. Some of them will return to Israel and to everlasting life,

but some will be resurrected to shame and everlasting contempt.

God says the good news will be boldly preached to the Jewish people:

> *And they that be wise shall shine as the*
> *brightness of the firmament; and they that*
> *turn many to righteousness as the stars*
> *for ever and ever* (Daniel 12:3).

Many Jews will come to an understanding:

> *But thou, O Daniel, shut up the words, and*
> *seal the book, even to the time of the*
> *end: many shall run to and fro, and*
> *knowledge shall be increased* (Daniel 12:4).

" . . . *many shall run to and fro, . . .* " means walking through the pages of the Bible with your fingers—the Jewish people will walk through the pages and understand prophetic statements of their Messiah. Knowledge will be increased, for they will know Him from the revelation of the Word and from the power of the Holy Spirit.

Next we read of the question asked by the angel to " . . . *the man clothed in linen, . . .* ":

137

NOTES

Then I Daniel looked, and, behold, there stood other two, the one on this side of the bank of the river, and the other on that side of the bank of the river. And one said to the man clothed in linen, which was upon the waters of the river, How long shall it be to the end of these wonders? (Daniel 12:5,6).

The One giving the answer is the great I AM, the Lion of the tribe of Judah:

And I heard the man clothed in linen, which was upon the waters of the river, when he held up his right hand and his left hand unto heaven, and sware by him that liveth for ever that it shall be for a time, times, and an half; and when he shall have accomplished to scatter the power of the holy people, all these things shall be finished (Daniel 12:7).

Now it is Daniel's turn to ask a question:

And I heard, but I understood not: then said I, O my Lord, what shall be the end of these things? (Daniel 12:8).

Note the length of time given in the answer which is similar to what we read in Revelation 10:1-6. We see the 3½ years that will be involved to finish God's plan for the Jews:

And he said, Go thy way, Daniel: for the words are closed up and sealed till the

138

time of the end. Many shall be purified, and made white, and tried; but the wicked shall do wickedly: and none of the wicked shall understand; but the wise shall understand. And from the time that the daily sacrifice shall be taken away, and the abomination that maketh desolate set up, there shall be a thousand two hundred and ninety days (Daniel 12:9-11).

A great inheritance is promised to Daniel in Daniel 12:12,13; he will stand in his lot at the end of the days:

Blessed is he that waiteth, and cometh to the thousand three hundred and five and thirty days. But go thou thy way till the end be: for thou shalt rest, and stand in thy lot at the end of the days.

In Joshua 14:2 we read that the casting of lots was how each tribe received its inheritance in the Promised Land. God has cast a lot for each of His children—a special inheritance. Daniel will stand in the inheritance that the Lord has for him in his glorified body. He will stand upon a plot of land that has been accounted his.

Jesus said that He would go away and prepare a place for us and come again and receive us unto Himself:

In my Father's house are many mansions: if it were not so, I would have told you. I go to prepare a place for you. And if I go and prepare a place for you, I will come again, and receive you unto myself; that where I am, there ye may be also (John 14:2,3).

We have a prepared lot—a prepared inheritance. Each of us is special in His sight. We shall rule and reign with Him forever and ever:

And there shall be no night there; and they need no candle, neither light of the sun; for the Lord God giveth them light: and they shall reign for ever and ever (Revelation 22:5).

NOTES

NOTES

There are three strong messages in the book of Daniel:

(1) God blesses in adversity.

(2) God rewards spiritual faithfulness.

(3) God disciplines nations.

Daniel was a righteous man:

> *Though these three men, Noah, Daniel, and Job, were in it, they should deliver but their own souls by their righteousness, saith the Lord GOD. Though Noah, Daniel, and Job, were in it, as I live, saith the Lord GOD, they shall deliver neither son nor daughter; they shall but deliver their own souls by their righteousness (Ezekiel 14:14,20).*

Daniel was a man greatly beloved:

> *At the beginning of thy supplications the commandment came forth, and I am come to shew thee; for thou art greatly beloved: therefore understand the matter, and consider the vision (Daniel 9:23).*

> *And he said unto me, O Daniel, a man greatly beloved, understand the words that I speak unto thee, and stand upright: for unto thee am I now sent. And when he had spoken this word unto me, I stood trembling (Daniel 10:11).*

> *And said, O man greatly beloved, fear not: peace be unto thee, be strong, yea, be strong. And when he had spoken unto me, I was strengthened, and said, Let my lord speak; for thou hast strengthened me (Daniel 10:19).*

Daniel's life ended as it had begun—in purpose, prayer, perception, and power.

NOTES

NOTES